The Architect's Garden

45 Original Landscapes

Lucy D. Rosenfeld

Schiffer Publishing Ltd
4880 Lower Valley Road, Atglen, Pa 19310

Library of Congress Control Number: 2008937588

Designed by RoS
Type set in Carleton/Zurich BT

ISBN: 978-0-7643-3130-5
Printed in China

Photo Credits: *Front cover:* design by Stefan Thuilot of Huettl Thuilot Associates; *back cover:* a design by Maria Smithburg of Artemesia; *title page:* a design by Hugh Durgan

Schiffer Books are available at special discounts for bulk purchases for sales promotions or premiums. Special editions, including personalized covers, corporate imprints, and excerpts can be created in large quantities for special needs. For more information contact the publisher:

Published by Schiffer Publishing Ltd.
4880 Lower Valley Road
Atglen, PA 19310
Phone: (610) 593-1777; Fax: (610) 593-2002
E-mail: Info@schifferbooks.com

For the largest selection of fine reference books on this and related subjects, please visit our web site at **www.schifferbooks.com**
We are always looking for people to write books on new and related subjects. If you have an idea for a book please contact us at the above address.

This book may be purchased from the publisher.
Include $5.00 for shipping.
Please try your bookstore first.
You may write for a free catalog.

In Europe, Schiffer books are distributed by
Bushwood Books
6 Marksbury Ave.
Kew Gardens
Surrey TW9 4JF England
Phone: 44 (0) 20 8392-8585; Fax: 44 (0) 20 8392-9876
E-mail: info@bushwoodbooks.co.uk
Website: www.bushwoodbooks.co.uk
Free postage in the U.K., Europe; air mail at cost.

Garden path by Rios, Clement, Hale (See Chapter 38)

Acknowledgements

I would like to thank the many architects and designers who contributed their work to this book. These imaginative people have made the design of garden space into a creative undertaking, and it has been a pleasure to write about each one. I would particularly like to acknowledge the help of architect Donald Mallow, and landscape architect, Gianni Biaggi. And, as always I thank my most faithful reader and supportive critic, my husband, Peter.

Contents

Introduction 7

Part I: Semi-Circles & Rectangles: Geometric Design Outside the Contemporary Home 10

1 • Donald Mallow, Architect 12
Contemporary Architecture Integrated With the Landscape

2 • Christoph Husler FSAP, Landscape Architect 14
A Panoramic Landscape with Geometric Accents

3 • Peter Kurt Woerner, Architect 17
Natural Beauty and Design Elegance

4 • Scott Lindenau A.I.A. and Kevin Heath A.I.A., Architects, Studio B Architects 19
Geometric Forms and Tranquility in the Shadow of a Mountain

Part II: Closer to Nature: Unusual Solutions for Waterside and Woodside Spaces 22

5 • Juergen Partridge, Architect 24
Seawalls and Terraces in a Waterside Landscape

6 • Antoine Predock, Architect 27
Contemporary Design Features a "Sky Ramp" for Birding

7 • Gavin Macrae-Gibson, Macrea-Gibson Architects 30
A Lakeside Vacation House Frames Its Views

8 • Elizabeth Thompson, Architect 34
An Ingenious Tree House for Children

9 • Steve Mensch, Architect 36
A Family Compound Preserves and Adapts to its Stunning Setting

10 • Grace Kennedy, Landscape Architect with Hanrahan and Meyers Architects 39
A Natural Landscape, Carefully Designed

Part III: The Dramatic Effect of Natural Stone 42

11 • Maria Smithburg of Artemesia, Landscape Architect 44
A Sunken Garden Outlined by Stone

12 • Juergen Partridge, Architect 47
Enjoying the Out -of -Doors in a Stony Woodland

13 • Mary Palmer Dargan, ASLA, Landscape Architect 49
A Stone Grotto at the Center of a Lush but Practical Design

14 • Sigrid Miller Pollin A.I.A. Architect, with Jane Thurber, Landscape Architect and Carol Pope, Landscape Designer 52
Stone Design Between Contemporary House and Meadow Beyond

15 • Donald Mallow, Architect 56
A Stone and Wooded Waterside Garden

16 • Milford Cushman, Architect, The Cushman Design Group, Inc. ... 59
Boulders and Terraces in a Green Mountain State Landscape

Part IV: An Added Dimension: Water Within the Garden 62

17 • Stefan Thuilot, Landscape Architect, Huettl-Thuilot Associates ... 64
Water Design Helps Define A Garden for Many Uses

18 • Marc Appleton, Architect 66
Spectacular Long Pool Reflects Canyon Vista Beyond

19 • Maria Smithburg, Artemesia, Landscape Architect; Tigerman McCurry Architects 70
Water Canals and Outlined Lawn in Geometric Design

20 • W + S Lansschaftsarchiteckten, Conceived by Toni Weber; Kerstin Godeke, Landscape Architect 74
Imaginative Water Design in a Meditative, Minimalist Garden

Part V: Intimate Spaces: Courtyards and Garden Rooms 78

21 • Michael G. Imber, Architect 80
An Oak-Canopied Cottage Courtyard

22 • Alexander Gorlin, Architect 83
Enclosed Garden Court Serves As an Oasis

23 • Stephen A. Tilly, Architect and Elizabeth Martin, Landscape Architect 87
A Romantic "Rusticated" Garden for a 19th Century Village Building

24 • Marc Appleton, Architect 89
When the Garden is the Inspiration

VI: Updating Traditional Garden Styles 92

25 • Hugh Dargan, ASLA, Landscape Architect 94
Garden "Rooms" with Old-World Charm and Present Day Uses

26 • Alexander Gorlin, Architect 97
Inspired by Ancient Rome: The Inviting Gardens of an Italianate House

27 • Michael Glassman, Archtitect 100
A Japanese Courtyard Garden for a U-Shaped House

28 • McIntosh Poris Associates, Architects 103
A Free Mason Symbol Reflected in an Oval Garden

29 • Michael G. Imber, Architect 106
Spanish Colonial Style for a Southwest Hunting Lodge

VII: Combining Fine Design, Sustainable Energy, and Environmental Smarts 108

30 • Ted Montgomery, Architect 110
Environmentally Sound, Aesthetically Pleasing Garden "Rooms"

31 • Line and Space Architects L.L.C. 112
A Desert Design with Protected Outdoor Areas

32 • Jennifer Siegal, Architect, Office of Mobile Design; James Stone, Land Design 114
Contemporary Design: Green, Recycled, and Chic

33 • Siegel and Strain, Architects 117
Keeping Cool with a Dogtrot

34 • Nathan Good AIA, Architect 119
Award-Winning "Green" Home with a Garden on the Roof

Part VIII: Art in the Garden: Combining Nature's Art with Sculpture 122

35 • Martin Lee Berlinger, Creative Gardens, Landscape Designer 124
Symbolic Asian Art and Plantings

36 • Steven Ehrlich, Architect; Nancy Goslee Power, Landscape Architect 128
Cubes, Angles, and Statuary in a Contemporary Setting

37 • Gianni Biaggi, Landscape Architect 131
A Swiss Garden Combining Tradition and Imaginative Sculpture

38 • Rios Clementi Hale Studios, Landscape Architects 133
Contemporary Sculpture Enhances a Garden Design

39 • Jon Piasecki of Golden Bough, Landscape Architect 136
A Naturalist Sculptor Designs a Landscape

40 • Blaise Bourgeois of Oxalis. Landscape Architect 138
When Nature Takes Sculptural Forms

IX: Defining Space with Pergolas, Arches, Gazebos, and Fences 142

41 • Elizabeth Thompson. Architect 145
Whimsical Gazebo Complements a Japanese Garden

42 • Stefan Thuilot with Joseph Huettl, Huettl-Thuilot Associates, Landscape Architects 147
Defining Structures in a Design for Outdoor Living

43 • Peter Kurt Woerner, Architect 150
An Old Meeting Hall's Garden Gets a Makeover

44 • Stephen Ahfl and Owner, Designers 152
Waterside Gazebo Overlooking a Wildlife Refuge

45 • Chris Schmitt of Schmitt Walker Architects and Thomas Angell of Verdant Enterprises, Landscape Architect 154
Innovative Wooden Constructions near a Salt Marsh

List of Architects and Landscape Designers 158

List of Photographers 160

Introduction

The word "garden" generally brings to mind an area next to a house with a green lawn and perhaps some flower or vegetable beds and borders. There might be a tree or two and perhaps an area for sitting. A garden is perhaps larger and more elegant than a "yard" and more private than a park, and if it is particularly grand might be characterized in the plural as "gardens." Many experts have written about how to plant such gardens, in a variety of traditional styles.

This, however, is not a book about how to plant, what soil to use, what shrubs will grow in a particular climate, or the concerns of the hands-on gardener. It is, rather, a study of the design of outdoor space—the gardens of our imaginations—and their relationship to architecture. For today's designers have expanded the traditional understanding of what space next to a house might look like. In so doing, they have created many new ideas for outdoor areas, combining the aesthetic, the practical, and the environmentally sound.

The idea of landscape and architecture working together is hardly a new one, of course. But contemporary structures have often stood alone in an empty landscape, like a precious gem set in a box to be admired. Today, more and more architects are designing the space around a house themselves, or working with landscape architects to create an aesthetic relationship between the house and garden. In some of the designs that follow garden design is by artists who work with nature; in others, unusual architectural design is related directly to the patterns of the garden.

In fact, some designers have chosen to avoid flowers and shrubbery entirely, in favor of "landscape perspectives," created by loggias and patios and other built structures. (One such example in this book is a spectacular water stairway.) In some of the following designs, planting is in pots rather than in the ground, allowing for continual change of color and ambiance. No matter what the design of the gardens in this collection, however, all are planned with harmony with the adjacent architecture in mind, whether arranged for avid birdwatchers, or lovers of art, or of seaside views, or people who like to live as much as possible out of doors.

Of course, the boundaries between indoor and outdoor living are often blurred in today's designs (particularly in clement climates). By creating inviting outdoor spaces, easily accessed (and viewed from within the house), and by continuing design elements from the architecture, these garden areas function like additional rooms, with colors, textures, framed views, and inviting layouts for entertaining, relaxing, and play.

Such designs must work not only with the architecture, but with the natural setting as well. Hillsides, flowing water, dry land, heavy winds—many natural elements may dictate how the area is designed and what materials and plantings can by used. In an area, for example, with lots of natural stone, it may become a prominent part of the plan, with piles of stone or distinctively placed boulders set into the landscape.

A major issue is when to leave the landscape in its natural state. The imposition of the architect's hand on the surroundings of the house is dealt with in a variety of interesting ways in the following projects—some opting to bring the wilderness closer, some to push it behind walls or fences, and others to use its native materials so that the more civilized garden will seem to blend gracefully into the wilderness beyond.

In order to arrive at a landscape plan, architects of the land and the people who will live in the house must agree on how it will be used. Practical considerations, such as shelter from the wind or sun for delicate plantings, or plants to reduce noise or provide privacy, or areas for children to play or other activities—these considerations must be weighed against purely aesthetic choices. Great views can dictate such decisions for the garden planner; a fine seaside vista, for example, might call for simplicity in the garden nearby. Maximizing light and air or shade might decide the issue of retaining or planting tall trees.

And, of course, the planning of the garden area for entertaining, pools, playgrounds, cooking areas, growing vegetables, or bird watching—among many other uses—means that the design of space is frequently divided into outdoor "rooms." These small divisions enable the designer to create areas with different colors, styles, seasonal plantings, and even garden structures to accommodate a variety of outlooks and interests. A variety of floors, tree canopies, walls, gateways, and pergolas are among the ways the designer can differentiate among the various garden rooms. Another is with a series of paths or fences and decorative walkways, which can continue the linear patterns of the architecture with curves and rectangles. Courtyards are among the most common smaller divisions, bordered on two or three sides by building, creating a sheltered, well-defined space for outdoor living and privacy. Hillsides, too, lend themselves to division with terraces on different levels providing an opportunity for unusual design.

Not all of today's gardens are modern in design, of course. Many people choose more formal rather than informal designs, using traditional styles of garden design, whether Asian or South Western or formal French, for example, but the challenges are similar. These more traditional styles must balance the formal with contemporary ideas and spatial relationships—in some ways a more difficult task than free-form garden layouts. Like interior designers creating a new version of a traditional setting, these garden architects face a variety of problems in updating the past for today's tastes. For example, traditional gardens often are characterized by symmetry—a concept that might seem somewhat dated to today's architects. How does the landscape designer create a formal layout without reverting to an old-fashioned, retro style?

Another major consideration is the "greening" of the space. Ecology-minded designers are seeking energy-efficient, sustainable solutions to outdoor design, just as they are for their indoor plans. Many innovative ideas, including roof gardens, re-circulating water, and the use of "found" materials (like bathtubs and storage bins) for planting are now being used in landscape architecture. The choice of drought-resistant or rain-tolerant plants is another way ecology-minded planners try to limit their impact on the environment.

For some art-lovers, a garden is a place for sculpture. The intersection of architecture, gardens, and art has a long and illustrious history. It is certainly of interest today, with sculpture prominently displayed in all kinds of settings. How does if fit into a contemporary landscape—what kind of surroundings are best for looking at art, or is the art merely a decorative addition to the plantings? Some designers see unusual structures as themselves a form of sculpture. Unusual gazebos and other small buildings and walls or fences are increasingly being used today to define space, or even to draw out elements of the architecture into the garden area.

And then, of course, there are the less tangible design choices: how to create the elements of surprise or intimacy or contemplative peace in the space allotted. These less-obvious decisions are made according to the personality and aesthetic sensibilities of the designers and tenants of the house. There are all kinds of shibboleths about garden design: that curves soften a landscape, for example, that trellises and other rectilinear structures create frames through which to view the garden, or that various colors of plantings set the mood of the garden. In the following pages you will see a great variety of garden spaces—and perhaps find the inspiration you might need to create an unusual garden of your own.

PART I: SEMI-CIRCLES & RECTANGLES:

Outdoor design for this elegant Connecticut house by Peter Kurt Woerner includes geometric arrangement of semi-circles. (See Chapter 3)

Geometric Design Outside the Contemporary Home

Strong geometric design has been a major element in architecture for decades, and many of today's garden and patio plans echo the strong lines, angles, and curves that characterize contemporary houses. The clear and precise lines of geometry have fascinated architects since the Bauhaus in the early twentieth century; today's designers have employed many of the same spatial relationships in the landscape surrounding their houses.

Using rectangles, grids, triangles, circles, and half-circles to lay out patio areas continues the architectural aesthetic of the building. The projects in this section are, of course, all different, but they share a taste for geometric design and geometric motifs, while extending the living area to the out-of-doors.

Rectangular terraces and pools reflect the aesthetic of a contemporary house by architect, Donald Mallow. In this example, there is a strong connection between the building's architecture and the layout of the outdoor living area —both in materials and design, with geometrically organized space punctuated by plantings and reflective water.

A hilly and panoramic Swiss landscape is organized with a combination of geometric outlines and free form plantings in the next project. Here horizontal lines and a large rectangular terrace predominate, but there are also angles and curves.

Curves, circles, and semi-circles are no less geometric than the rectangles seen in these designs. Architect Peter Kurt Woerner uses a series of arched shapes to echo and delineate both the marsh side of the Connecticut house he designed, and its striking curved deck and pool area. Here a series of curves carry the eye from house to outdoor areas, to protective wall.

A particularly geometric design characterizes architect Scott Lindenau's Colorado house. The dynamic vertical lines and flat roof are reflected in the rectilinear layout of the patio—a contrast with the rolling mountain lines not far away.

In all of these projects, the composition of house and outdoor space suggests twentieth century geometric abstract painting, with Mondrian-like attention to balance, rhythm, line fragments, and repeated squares and motifs.

1 • Donald Mallow, Architect

Contemporary Architecture Integrated With the Landscape

New Jersey

In this imposing design, the contemporary house is extended into outdoor living space without breaking the aesthetic sensibility; its architecture and landscaping are inseparable. The layout of the terraces, pools, and gardens behind the house is fully integrated with the architecture of the building itself.

The terraces, which adjoin the house (and are easily viewed from indoors through large expanses of glass mitered at the corners), provide a spacious area for outdoor living. Not only does the landscape design echo the patterns and geometric shapes and forms of the architecture, but the materials used carry over into the terrace design. Even the pools (one circular for carp, one rectangular for swimming) reflect the lines and forms of the house. The carp pool is the only round form in the layout, punctuating the angular design of its surroundings.

The materials of the house—primarily concrete and stone—with flooring of Alta Quartzite, are used outside as well. Douglas fir is found in both the interior (ceilings) and exterior (soffits), while painted steel is used in structural forms. Balconies are cantilevered over the terrace. The geometrically arranged terraces and garden areas are defined by low concrete walls capped by six inch thick bluestone. Areas for planting are built into the landscape design and provide a welcome touch of color.

The continuation of a house's architecture into the outdoor area creates an enlarged living area, with the out-of-doors becoming an extension of the house itself. Wild nature is at a distance, with the house and its outdoor area characterized by a sense of order and balance, as well as elegance.

Above left:
Cantilevered balconies overhang pool and terrace area, as seen from above.

Below left:
Geometric patterns in terraces reflect architectural forms and materials of the house.

Right:
At dusk, architecture of house is reflected in pools.

2 • Christoph Husler FSAP, Landscape Architect

A Panoramic Landscape with Geometric Accents

Blonay, Switzerland

In this panoramic, hilly Swiss landscape, we focus on the design of the space near the late 19th century house (lived in for many years by noted composer Paul Hindemith, and now housing the Hindemith Foundation). The grounds have recently been updated and redesigned. The new look includes terraces and arbors, a hillside lawn, a rock garden, a garden of shade, garden steps, and a row of linden trees. The layout for these features has free-form areas of plantings amid a general aspect of geometric design, with dominant horizontal lines.

In 2002 the garden was in a state of neglect when landscape architect, Christoph Husler, undertook its renovation. The new design included restoring the panoramic terrace, which forms a large rectilinear area near the house, with plantings on the sides and low, dry stone walls framing the open area, and accenting the horizontal lines. There is even a circle shape for contrast: a large circular arbor for roses is placed at one end of the terrace. A plane tree, pruned into a slab-like form, provides shade near the house.

A hedge of boxwoods forms another straight line at the crest of the hill, with a low terrace wall creating a visible V-shaped angle set into the hillside. There is a wooden gazebo with small diamond-shaped latticework that frames the view with its rectangular opening. The entrance driveway is bordered by a row of linden trees, pruned into horizontal planes; their pruning keeps the vista clear from the house (they also provide shade for people walking up the hill). This is a landscape design that seems natural to its site, while using geometric—primarily horizontal—accents in its organization.

Wooden gazebo frames view with rectangular opening and small diamond shapes of latticework.

Horizontal lines are prevalent in the row of linden trees near the driveway, and in the long terrace, with contrasting circular arbor at one end.

Rectilinear lines of the panoramic terrace are outlined by low stone walls and flower plantings along the edges, while a wall with a V-shaped angle contrasts on hill above.

Late 19th century house atop a hilly landscape has newly renovated gardens and long entrance drive.

3 • Peter Kurt Woerner, Architect

Natural Beauty and Designed Elegance

Connecticut

Picturesquely situated on a granite ledge above a great salt marsh, this architect's Connecticut home has five half-levels, encompassing living space, two studios, dining area in a greenhouse (providing solar energy), and a balcony looking out to the water below. The house has a shingled exterior, in keeping with New England tradition, and it is surrounded by native trees and salt marsh vegetation.

While the house has a naturally tranquil scenic setting, its designed outdoor spaces have a dramatic and contemporary look. This design is based, according to the architect, "on an unusual configuration—basically a half-circle, that starts at the ledge on one side and arches over to the other side." The use of curves is central to the plan—both of the house and the outdoor areas.

The front, public side of the deck is protected from view by a sinuous, solid wall, while the far side is open to a serene view of the marshes just beyond. A geometric pattern of curves appears in both the house and surroundings: the spectacular pool and adjoining deck reflect the rounded lines of the house.

The architect's garden is in a solar heated greenhouse that is also a dining area; this house, its indoor garden, and its outdoor area have a careful arrangement of angles and curves that frame and emphasize the natural beauty all around.

This architect's garden is in a solar heated greenhouse that is also a dining area, emphasizing natural beauty both indoors and out

Spectacularly sited shingled, contemporary house rests on a granite ledge over salt marsh.

Designs for pool, deck, and pool house create interesting geometric pattern, while echoing curving lines of the house.

Marsh side of pool is open to view of rocks and water beyond.

4 • Scott Lindenau AIA, Studio B Architects; Kevin Heath AIA, Project Manager

Geometric Forms and Tranquility in the Shadow of a Mountain

Colorado

This contemporary home and outdoor courtyard area emphasize rectilinear forms, in contrast with the curving lines of the mountain view not far away. Its terrace space suggests an outdoor room facing the vista beyond. The house is only one story high, so as not to compete with the wilderness view in the distance.

With the property adjacent to a highway, the architects chose to build a 22-inch rammed earth wall to act as a sound barrier and protection from highway lights on the street side. Nestled behind the wall are an elegant house, courtyard, and garden, creating for its residents a sense both of enclosure and openness to the beautiful view beyond. Designed primarily with rectangular forms, both house and its outdoor area use similar materials. Exterior components, along with reddish-colored rammed earth, are rusted steel vertical panels, aluminum window and door systems, and honed granite. Long windows and a grid-like exterior on the deck side emphasize geometric elements. There is a shallow, rectangular reflecting pool surrounded by a comfortable sitting and dining area, as well as stepping stones, and a hot tub. Contemporary deck furniture and two small elephant statues complete the décor of this outdoor room.

Whether in the snowy Colorado winter or in the summer swimming season, this project creates a sense of order and an attractive environment for outdoor activities.

Nestled against house in back is elegant area for outdoor living in warmer weather.

Geometric elements of house are picked up in rectangular designs of courtyard, and form contrast with rolling mountain line beyond.

Shallow reflecting pool has pebbles and stepping stones.

The house has rammed earth walls on street side, mountain view behind it.

Part II: Closer to Nature:

Reaching out to nature in the form of a 60-foot suspension bridge from vacation home to natural landscape, in a design by Macrae-Gibson. (See Chapter 11)

Many projects aim to incorporate natural surroundings, rather than to formalize them, or separate living spaces from them. For those designs that reach out to waterfront or woodlands, the focus is on enjoying the natural setting, whether as glorious "framed" views, or as nearby spaces to use for sports, entertaining or bird watching.

Settings such as these are highly prized, and the designer is faced with a somewhat different set of problems: instead of creating an outdoor environment from empty space, he or she must work with nature's ready-made design, whether tidal basin, forest ravine, or lakefront.

Waterfront properties are the most coveted. The garden designer who works with a space that includes oceanfront, or a rushing river and waterfall, or a tranquil lake or salt-marsh need not worry about focal points and bringing interest to the site. A water view is almost always greatly beloved and central to the design of the landscape.

In many cases the waterfront is a short distance from the house, so the plan may include walkways and docks, but even if the nearby shore is merely a brilliant view rather than a viable access for boating or swimming, the architect frames it and incorporates it into the design. In fact, whether the water is rushing or tidal or tranquil and serene, the garden

Unusual Solutions for Waterside and Woodside Spaces

design cannot seem to compete with it. The glamorous waterfall or heavy surf provide ever-changing motion, sound, and color—the designs of nature—that would make complex garden design seem fussy and superfluous. And if the waterfront is tranquil and grand, reflecting sky and changing with the wind, the garden must leave room for contemplative enjoyment of it grandeur. For those projects that are on the edge of beautiful woodlands, decisions about encroaching on the forest and disturbing the habitat of birds and indigenous trees and plants are equally important.

The architects chosen in the following pages have all worked with natural surroundings, and have tried to incorporate the spectacular settings into their plans. One of the most striking projects is by Juergen Partridge of Ontario. His waterside landscape includes a series of terraces and a seawall that adjoin Lake Ontario in spectacular fashion. With its native white stone and lush plantings. the steep hillside to the lake is transformed without obscuring the blue lake at its edge.

A different sort of natural landscape is found in the magnificent setting of woods and waterfall that surround architect Steve Mensch's compound in New York's Hudson valley. Having found a property with a spectacular natural landscape, the architect designed the space near the house with walkways, natural rock outcroppings, and a suspension bridge to bring nature closer, but not to compete with the glamorous environment.

Architect Antoine Predock also used a bridge to nature in his New Mexico design for a bird watching client. His triangular "sky-ramp" reaches over a ravine into the wooded landscape from the house like a giant ship's prow, bring nature closer to the house without disturbing.

One way to get closer to natural beauty is to settle up in the trees themselves. Architect Elizabeth Thompson's tree house does just that, bringing small visitors up a ladder to a well-designed structure high above the garden below.

The island in a lake design by architect Gavin Macrae-Gibson is another notable solution to bringing natural beauty closer. This project, overlooking a pristine Canadian lake, includes a sixty-foot suspension bridge over the woods below and down to the shoreline. The house design is punctuated with tree limbs and small branches salvaged from the spot and used to frame the beautiful views all around—a kind of symbolic tie from home to landscape.

Landscape architect Grace Kennedy has designed an area around a house that is situated within an already lush, wooded area. By choosing and planting trees and shrubbery to surround the structure, she brings natural beauty right to the doors of the house.

5 • Juergen Partridge, Architect

Seawalls and Terraces in a Waterside Landscape

Ontario

"An exercise in modern engineering and creativity," this property on the banks of Lake Ontario provides both safety and aesthetic beauty in an award-winning and spectacular landscape. Working with a steep cliff face on the edge of the lake, the architect began with a thirty-foot sea wall, and worked upwards with a multi-terraced layout that includes a boat house, pool, a waterfall, a hot tub, a dock and even an outdoor fireplace. There is even a putting green.

Natural stone steps lead up from water's edge to a boathouse surrounded by greenery. On the lower tier of the terraces is an organically shaped gunite pool, which receives a steady flow of water from a thirty-foot waterfall. The pool is surrounded by a flagstone sitting area and lush plantings.

Armour stone is used for upper terraces, which are devoted to plantings, seating, and entertaining. On the upper level, the freestanding outdoor fireplace and hot tub are added amenities, nearer to the house itself. A quaint, gently arched bridge with iron railings is an additional picturesque feature.

This architect's project in a cold, but glamorous, setting brings the beauties of nature right to the edge of the house. The residents can enjoy the out-of-doors right on their own doorstep at any time of year—whether from the lakeside, or one of the many terraces, or as views of a beautiful waterside landscape through the windows of the house.

On the banks of Lake Ontario, this spectacular stone and greenery landscape covers a steep slope up to the house.

An organically shaped swimming pool and lounge area are on a lower level of the terraced design.

Free-standing outdoor fire place is one of many amenities for enjoying outdoor living.

Waterfront level has putting green, boathouse, and dock.

6 • Antoine Predock, Architect

Contemporary Design Features a "Sky-Ramp" for Birding

New Mexico

One of the most extraordinary solutions to the problems of bringing nature and home closer together is noted architect Antoine Predock's Turtle Creek House in Albuquerque, New Mexico. Here, a glass, stainless steel, and limestone construction literally reaches out into the New Mexico landscape, creating both a striking design and a bird watcher's paradise.

The house has a limestone front made of ledges with native plantings, which suggest a "timeless relationship" to the nearby geologic Austin chalk formation. Behind the house a ravine is literally bridged by a sloping "sky ramp," that reaches into different bird habitats: water's edge, foliage, understory, and to the sky itself. This great steel bridge allows the bird watching owners of the house to "walk into nature," while a triangular grassy seating area, or "prow" sits below it.

Reflection is another element the architect used to conjoin the contemporary home and its natural surroundings. A curving, twenty-foot square, convex, polished stainless steel piece at the back of the house reflects the greenery nearby, and the architectural characteristics of the building.

This thoroughly contemporary building suggests that avian habitats and native stone and natural greenery can comfortably coexist with the most modern of architectural ideas.

Below the ramp is a triangular seating "prow" set into a grassy terrace.

Polished stainless steel creates reflection of natural surroundings.

A "sky-ramp" stretches into nearby greenery and avian habitat for bird-watching owners.

The front of the house has anchoring limestone ledges relating it tonearby geologic formation.

7 • Gavin Macrae-Gibson, Macrae-Gibson Architects

A Lakeside Vacation House Frames Its Views

Quebec

This magnificently set vacation home on an island in a Canadian lake is reached by boat in summer, and by car driving over the ice in winter. The steeply gabled log house is approached from a wharf by a boardwalk and a sixty-foot suspension bridge. All around are the beautiful natural woods of the Laurentian Mountain area, with their plentiful silver birches, cedars, fir, and ash trees. Fields of ferns, iris, lupin, and lavender lead down to a nearby stream. The natural beauty of these surroundings has been left intact.

So that the occupants can enjoy the great views and unspoiled habitat, the house has screened porches on three sides that frame the vistas just beyond. Verandas such as these become a kind of transition to the outdoors, a link between the wooden construction of the house and the woods beyond. A rope suspension bridge to a guesthouse near the lakeside adds to the impression that the house is "floating above the lake," rather than being anchored by a large quantity of steps.

To further the idea of combining the man-made structure with nature, the architect has used trees (ash and maple) from the site for ballustrading, decks, and furniture. Some ash trees—with branches intact—form part of the composition of decks, railings and interiors.

These trees are symbolic of the strong connection between the architectural design and its surroundings; their use on the verandas literally creates frames for each view of the lake and forest. This is truly a merging of architecture and nature in a spectacular setting.

Deck overlooking lake has an ash tree that once grew on the site as a support; its branches are used for railings.

Many-gabled log vacation house has great verandas and a rope suspension bridge.

Left:
Expansive verandas frame lakeside views.

Center:
Natural forest growth and wildflowers are left intact around house and guest cottage.

Right:
Wood and stone interiors use natural tree forms as well.

8 • Elizabeth Thompson, Architect

An Ingenious Tree House for Children

New York

Most outdoor settings are designed for grown-ups. This unusual project is for the kids; here a plexi-glass, cedar, and stainless steel, screened tree house sits high in the trees on a Long Island property. (The adults have a shingled house, with its own pleasing nooks and crannies, as well as flower gardens and lawns.)

The tree house, in a small forested area overlooking an apple orchard, is slightly removed from the house, but it is wonderfully separate. As the architect says, "Up with the birds and breezes, the tree house gently sways...a tree house is a metaphor for a bucolic escape from the everyday stresses in life..." The tree house is designed and scaled for children, a place for "contemplations of the world below," or a lunchtime outing, or an afternoon game of chess or checkers. More intrepid children can even spend the night in the trees.

The structure is built in a rustic style, its weathered supports matching the beech tree trunks that adjoin it. It is almost hidden by greenery, adding to its magical sense of isolation. The roof and sides of the house are built of translucent white plexi-glass, which reflects the tones of trees and sky. There is fiberglass screening for buggy times. A ladder stretches up to the opening, and a bucket for provisions can be lowered.

Both rustic-seeming and architecturally sophisticated, this miniature house is about as close to nature as one can get—literally sited among the leaves and birds of the forest.

A wooded walkway adjoins the shingled Long Island home.

Charming, rustic tree house is perched amid beech trees not far from the house.

White, translucent fiberglass panels cover sides; access is by ladder and opening in the floor of this hidden aerie.

Screening stretches above fiberglass panels for protection at buggy times.

9 • Steve Mensch, Architect

A Family Compound Preserves and Adapts to Its Stunning Setting

New York

A compound of several houses, studios, and bridges, this project is deep in the heart of the scenic Hudson valley. The property of hundreds of acres has the elements so beloved by the Hudson River painters a century and a half ago: a deep kill (or creek), a fifty-foot waterfall, ponds, a dam, huge outcroppings of rock, and dense forest all around.

The design of the man-made elements preserves and frames the natural beauty around it. Houses for family members are reached by boardwalks and two foot-bridges—one a suspension bridge across the kill above the falls. A loop of gardens and trails meanders through the property. There is an outdoor kitchen and eating area, a lawn and a pool and pool house for everyone's use, but each house is separate and invisible from the others, in order to preserve privacy and the landscape itself.

The gardens are woodland gardens, with rhododendrons, mountain laurel, dogwood, ferns, amid white birches and other native trees. Outcroppings of rock—some natural to the site, and some brought in—define the spaces and differentiate natural wooded areas from planted gardens.

Of course, the dramatic waterfall is the scenic wonder of the setting. For great views the architect built a pavilion at an angle to the dam; its sides can be opened up so it functions as kind of umbrella over the rock ledge and the thundering falls. Pavilions, decks, balconies, and a long boardwalk all contribute to the family's ability to be near the natural wonders that surround them.

Suspension bridge goes across kill and from one house to another—all hidden from view by the forest.

Aerial view of Hudson River valley setting shows dense forest and waterfall.

The house sits beside spectacular waterfall.

Boardwalks wind through the compound in the woods.

Outcroppings of rock differentiate garden and forest spaces near the house.

10 • Grace Kennedy, Landscape Architect; Hanrahan and Meyers, Architects

A Natural Landscape, Carefully Designed

New York

Located in a wooded, gently hilly area of the Hudson valley, this contemporary weekend house by Hanrahan and Meyers, Architects, sits comfortably in its old and new surroundings. Landscape Architect Grace Kennedy has planted a profusion of trees and shrubbery, and designed the area with an eye to line, color, and texture, as well as to the geometric architecture of the recently constructed house.

These aesthetic choices mask a series of practical decisions; she has chosen plantings that will stem hillside erosion and contribute to drainage, or deter deer, or camouflage the air conditioning unit, in addition to creating beauty around it. A turf roof covers the garage to help with insulation. She has planted many berry bushes (including blueberries and bayberries) to encourage birds.

From a visual standpoint, many of the plantings are set out in undulating curves to complement the angular planes of the house, including a snake design of berry bushes and grasses on the ridges of a nearby low hill. The choice of flowers and blooming shrubbery is related to fields or units of color; some of the plantings are even chosen to create changing shadow play on a wall of the house. Texture is also a consideration, with each tree or shrub chosen for its own properties.

Although this project was built into an already wooded area, the newer plantings bring nature right to the doors of the house—but it is nature carefully designed and nurtured, and practically, as well as aesthetically, conceived.

Color matters in this design: the hill garden features white dogwoods; most of the flowers planted here are white, blue or very light yellow. Near the house are fragrant sumac, river birch, witch hazel and bayberry; all the foliage is green.

Newly built house is surrounded by ferns and fragrant sumac, massed below delicate witch hazel.

A stone wall is next to turf roof of the garage. The curving planting bed follows a dry riverbed...

Undulating plantings of grass and blueberries snake across lawn in front of the house, while view toward pool house includes stone path, "small sculptural trees," and lawn.

... both accommodating drainage and creating contrast with angularity of house.

Part III: The Dramatic Effect of Natural Stone:

Native stone walls create interesting patterns, punctuated with pots and flowers in this garden by Maria Smithburg of Artemesia. (See Chapter 11)

A setting of great boulders or a romantic, ivy-covered stone wall are just two of the ways native stone can be used to enhance garden design. Native stone is both a glamorous and practical solution to all kinds of design enigmas—it is certainly sturdy, aesthetically attractive, usually abundantly available on site, and always natural looking. As a visual addition it can be used to create a free-form environment, or geometric boundaries, as a dramatic background for plantings or waterfalls, or as an added dimension of color and texture. It can relate the garden area directly to the materials of the adjoining house, or create a contrast to the delicacy of flowers or shrubbery. From a practical standpoint, it can protect against erosion or water run-off, provide privacy, and create a variety of natural environments around it.

In the following designs the use of stone ranges from the most civilized of roles to the wildest—for no two projects look anything alike. Nonetheless, they all share an affinity for this natural element.

In the first project landscape designer Maria Smithburg of Artemesia used a pattern of intersecting stone walls on different levels in the design of her sunken Colorado garden—a most unusual solution to a sloping terrain. Her use of stone walls creates a garden designed like a geometric work of art.

Juergen Partridge, in the next project, creates a more free-form landscape with its use of native stone. This Ontario hideaway uses natural outcroppings of stone as the dramatic setting for a waterfall near a cottage in the woods.

Landscape designer, Mary Palmer Dargan, uses granite in a lush romantic setting. A twelve-foot high granite wall controls hillside erosion, but the stone wall also forms an essential part of a romantic garden design, complete with grotto.

Architect Sigrid Miller Pollin bridges the area between contemporary house and hay meadow beyond by using stone. In her design, a granite patio and a variety of unusual shapes create " a person-made landscape" as a transition to the natural beauty nearby.

Boulders native to the Maine landscape are carefully set in architect Donald Mallow's garden down to a salt marsh. These large stones seem utterly natural to the site, but are actually used for steps, terracing and pathways.

Perhaps the most stone-oriented of these designs is by Milford Cushman of Vermont; his stony New England landscape glories in the native boulders and stream beds, using the stone both in walls and steps and its natural tumbling shapes.

11 • Maria Smithburg of Artemesia, Landscape Architect

A Sunken Garden Outlined by Stone

Colorado

Situated on a sloping hillside amid the graceful white aspens for which its town is named, this house and garden have a unique layout—one that is intended "to move with the terrain" and "to make the landscape unfold in abstract patterns," according to the designer. The house is bordered by a field of wild flowers, a forest of aspens, and a most unusual sunken garden. Large amounts of glass in the house make the landscape visible and immediate.

Stone predominates in both house and garden. The house has a mostly stone exterior, with a flagstone walkway and an unusual rock "spillway" separating it from the garage and the field of wildflowers. Into this lovely setting, the designer has placed the unusual garden area.

The sunken garden features a series of quite closely set, parallel stone walls on several different levels, with various plantings carefully placed between them. Made of native Colorado stone, the walls have a natural reddish-brown color. Along with the white vertical lines of the aspen wood, these horizontal walls create an interesting design not unlike a modern geometric painting, culminating in a free-form rock spillway at the garden's edge, near the open filed of wild flowers and the aspen wood.

This unusual solution to creating a garden on sloping terrain is both practical and original; the walls of the garden function elegantly in aesthetic terms, as well as producing a sense of order and balance that contrasts with the natural beauty of field and forest all around.

Curving entrance steps to the house are made of warm-toned flagstone.

Above:
"Spillway" of rock separates house and garage and makes free-form sculpture adjacent to field of wildflowers.

Above, left:
Nearby Aspen woods can be clearly seen through large glass windows of stone house.

Below, left:
Unusual design of sunken garden is visible from within the house, with the forest just beyond.

Closely set walls of native Colorado stone and water-filled areas create interest patterns in sunken garden.

12 • Juergen Partridge, Architect

Enjoying the Out-of-Doors in a Stony Woodland

Ontario

Since there is only one room in this hideaway in the Canadian woods, the out-of-doors is especially important. This charming, award-winning project known as Celtic Cottage, makes use of its surroundings in a particularly appealing way; Celtic characteristics "were paramount" to the owners, and classic Celtic ornamentation was used (note the fireplace decorations).

The house is a comparatively simple frame construction, nestled into a beautiful wilderness setting, only feet from the tumbling waterfall. The waterfall spilling over free-form boulders in the clearing are natural elements; the designer added a picturesque wood trellis and an original outdoor fireplace. Residents can enjoy outdoor cooking and dining; the fireplace is used even in snowy Canadian winters.

The great series of stone boulders is the major element of the exterior design, providing both sight and sound of the natural landscape. This is a project that uses stone as the centerpiece of its landscape.

Traditional Celtic design can be found throughout, including on the fireplace.

Charming cottage in the woods has its own waterfall.

Residents enjoy outdoor cooking and eating outdoors, with use of picturesque and practical stone fireplace.

13 • Mary Palmer Dargan ASLA, Landscape Architect

A Stone Grotto at the Center of a Lush but Practical Design

North Carolina

Combining a romantic beauty with practical considerations, this pretty garden is a fine example of using a difficult setting well. At a 4000-foot elevation in western North Carolina, the garden is only twenty-four feet wide and sits at the base of a steep hillside. It is subject to severe winds and water run-off, and needs protections from the slope beyond.

The landscape design was seen as a "transition from steep hillside to house." But the garden appears both spacious and inviting, due to its unusual configuration of curves, bits of wall, and seating areas that break up its long, rectangular shape.

Edging the profuse plantings and a sitting area, is a great twelve-foot high wall made of enormous granite rocks reclaimed from a monument company. They were cut by hand to fit on this site. The centerpiece of this huge wall is the charming grotto that helps give the garden its romantic aura.

Terraces, a waterfall niche, a potting shed, and other amenities and adornments are combined with extensive plantings in the lush garden. But behind the wall "sustainable techniques" and other practical considerations are included: drainage from the steep hill is created with earthen ties, and water wicks between the stones of the wall create a natural environment for growing (including volunteer species such as paulonia, "that have begun to colonize the great wall").

Although this garden was created only a few years ago, its layout, its particular plantings, and the use of stone give it a must older, more romantic look than many new gardens.

Garden is configured with curves and circles and a variety of design elements to break up its long, rectangular shape.

Lush garden of stone details and attractive plantings is adjacent to the house, with high wall as a border.

Grotto is part of 12-foot high wall, protecting the garden from wind and water run-off, and providing decorative, romantic aura.

Profuse plantings surround grotto, as well as growing between the granite blocks that make up the wall and grotto.

14 • Sigrid Miller Pollin, AIA, Architect, with Jane Thurber, Landscape Architect, and Carol Pope, Landscape Designer

Stone Design Between Contemporary House and Meadow Beyond

Massachusetts

This striking contemporary house has just been completed; its unusual curving roofline suggests its setting in a picturesque New England landscape of rolling hills and meadows. Designed as a live/work environment, the house is both aesthetically dramatic and ecologically practical.

Though the house itself is made of white cedar wood (in a nod to Massachusetts' traditional white wooden frame houses), its exterior setting uses several types of stone for its patio and driveway areas. The stone areas function both as visual transitions to the large hay fields below, and as intimate spaces for outdoor living near the house. The stone designs feature light-colored, local "Goshen stone," named for a nearby town where it is mined. The patio is made up of irregularly shaped pieces of stone and granite cobblestones. The deck walls are transparent tempered glass with slender aluminum posts to blend into the landscape. " There is a constant relationship between the landscape and the built environment," says the architect.

The large entry courtyard with granite benches is defined on two sides by the structure, and on the other sides by trees and shrubs, providing privacy and enclosed space for gardening. She sees the "built" garden as an extension of the meadow beyond; there are ornamental grasses, Russian sage, geraniums and yarrow, among other plants. An arbor for shade plants is located near the low point of the roof curve. Goshen stone is also used for retaining walls and a stairway, with plantings on the edges.

This area "is intended to be a person-made landscape," says the architect, "a colorful landscape of perennials and varying ground covers, it acts as a counterpoint to the expansive view of the natural terrain."

Play of curves in granite cobblestone entry driveway design echoes those in roof line and retaining walls.

The view to the east, framed by a window, is of spacious hay meadows and a forest.

The house has a distinctive curving roof line, suggesting the hills and meadows beyond. An arbor for shade plants is located beneath the low point of the curve.

Goshen stone (a light colored rock mined in Massachusetts) is used for stone bench, retaining wall, and stairway, with plantings on the edges.

Patio floor is characterized by irregular shapes of granite.

15 • Donald Mallow, Architect

A Stone and Wooded Waterside Garden

Maine

The site of this charming garden is truly a natural delight. But while its setting on a steep slope down to a salt-pond in Maine is natural, the garden did not "come" that way. Its design was created and implemented with indigenous rocks and native plantings—all chosen and placed with natural beauty in mind. Its site, a sloping area between a studio and the water, provides both a picturesque view from the studio windows, and a delightful place to enjoy the out-of-doors.

The native stone boulders are all around in coastal Maine, and the architect used them to terrace the garden into three tiers, and to delineate a path to the water, as well as for steps and accents. Maine perennials were densely planted in with natural growth, amid native pines and birches. The effect is one of free-form, accidental beauty. Small grassy areas were created near the shoreline. Small climbing plants grow and flower on the rocks.

This seasonal, carefully designed garden captures the tranquility and natural beauty of its setting; with the freely placed boulders and seemingly wild garden, the architect's hand is invisible.

Architect's Maine garden is on steep slope down to a salt pond.

Native boulders are used to terrace garden and to create steps and accents.

Combination of native Maine growth and planted perennials interspersed with natural rock makes garden seem completely natural.

16 • Milford Cushman, Architect, Cushman Design Group

Boulders and Terraces in a Green Mountain State Landscape

Vermont

With great stone walls, a patio, natural rock accents, and a tumbling brook over natural stone formations, this Vermont home fits beautifully into its surroundings. Rock is native to the northern New England landscape, as evidenced by the hundreds of stone walls built by early farmers and still seen throughout the state. Today some designers are using similar new stone walls, as well as free-form boulder groupings set in imaginative ways. In fact, dry stone walls (built without mortar to accommodate Vermont's dramatic freeze and thaw) can be seen in a number of recent landscape designs in the state.

This house is nestled into a landscape of walls and indigenous greenery. The angular planes of the house are reflected in the zigzag of the wall; the light color of the roof and the native stone accent the geometric forms of the house. Rather than formalizing the landscape, the design is free and natural looking, with stone used in a variety of ways, combining curves and straight lines and tumbling piles. A small rushing brook makes its way over more rocks, while a small sitting area is edged with piles of boulders. This deceptive juxtaposition of right angled walls, paths, stairs, and patios with natural rock formations makes the over-all design seem free-flowing and inviting to strollers, outdoor diners, and hikers—and anyone who enjoys the Vermont out-of-doors.

Stone is endemic to Vermont and the design uses it in many ways: walkways, a patio with dining area, and in the attractive irregular stair.

A combination of free form rock formations and geometric walls creates an inviting landscape.

More formal use of stone, as in geometric walls or this small sitting area, is combined with great boulders throughout the grounds.

A typically Vermont scene near the house captures the Green Mountain State's natural beauty, with a brook running over native rock under the trees.

Part IV: An Added Dimension:

Rotating fountain in California garden by Stefan Thuilot has corner spouts surrounded by bluestone and ornamental grasses. (See Chapter 17)

Water Features Within the Garden

Whether gently trickling from a fountain, rushing downward in a waterfall, or calmly reflecting the sky from a tranquil pond—water is the added dimension in many architect's gardens. Water features vary widely, but are always an eye-catching element of the design, creating motion, reflections, and surprise. The sound of moving water is like music to many people, adding dimension and appeal to a landscape. Not to be confused with shore gardens, where the view to ocean or lake is a more distant element, in-garden water features are often focal points surrounded by natural plantings and the use of stone or wood structures. (Some examples of natural landscapes with water views or shorelines appear in Part II.)

Water features in gardens have been around for a long time, in the form of ornamental lakes and falls, canals, and elegant fountains, usually in the design of large estates and public parks. Nowadays, decorative water designs are used frequently in smaller spaces as ornamental additions to an enclosed area.

With today's engineering feats, water can be used decoratively almost anywhere, and can be made to trickle or rush or disappear into a pile of rocks. It can be kept fresh and clean, as in a swimming pool, recycled, and used for growing plants. The trajectory of streams and canals can be designed by the architect to echo architectural elements in the house itself, with straight lines, or in contrast, with serpentine canals. A circular pond or a terraced garden's stream downward is a major sensory addition for both eye and ear, emphasizing a hilly terrain and creating a mood: romantic, formal, meditative, dramatic.

In the following projects water is indeed the added dimension to the garden plan.

Water is the unifying element in a garden for many uses, designed by Stefan Thuilot of Huettl-Thuilot Associates. A fountain with a rectangular basin and a wading pool are central elements of a complex, but tranquil layout of a California garden.

A dramatic landscape involving water is architect, Marc Appleton's, sixty-foot lap pool that is bordered by wood columns and tile designs, creating a spectacular landscape of reflective blue water, against a bright colored house.

Another use of waterways with sharply articulated straight edges characterizes a garden in Colorado, designed by Maria Smithburg of Artemesia. In this project narrow water canals are reflective accents that emphasize the geometric design of house and patio (by Tigerman McCurry, Architects), and separate the plantings from the patio in a jewel-like edging.

In a minimalist garden in Switzerland conceived by Toni Weber for W + S Landschaftarchitekten, and designed by Kerstin Godeke, water is used in an unusual and inspiring way. Here it tumbles over an asymmetrical staircase into a pond below in a steady and delicate movement, certainly the focus point of the landscape.

17 • Stefan Thuilot, Landscape Architect, Huettle Thuilot Associates

Water Design Helps Define a Garden For Many Uses

California

The aim of this award-winning design was to build upon the individual character—and use for—many different spaces, while unifying the property as a whole. The solution was to divide the garden into different sections, some for play, others for entertaining, or gardening—but to produce a consistency of design throughout.

To achieve this design aim, the plan involved a combination of similar materials—particularly bluestone paving—and the use of water as an element of design. The plan included a patio for entertaining, a large lawn for play, a garden area, a woodland to one side, and a front meadow. Square and custom-built bluestone was used for the patio and pathways, while a blue-aggregate concrete covered the front walk and back curb walls. A circular sandbox/fire pit and a variety of ornamental plantings soften this geometric emphasis. Throughout the design, strong horizontal lines of walls and pathways are punctuated with vertical white birch trees.

Water, however, is a major design element. The terrace wraps two sides of a fountain of smooth-cast concrete. The upper rectangular basin of a fountain is rotated so that copper spouts on two sides face both lawn and patio. An angled bluestone path runs through the patio, and surprisingly, is matched by the same pattern running underwater in a shallow section of a wading pool.

All through this layout, water and grassy areas are interspersed, creating a sense of space and tranquility, for the trickling fountain and the pool area are reflective and calming elements of the overall design.

Ornamental grasses punctuate the garden layout.

Left:
Fountain of smooth cast concrete has rotating basin with copper spouts on two sides.

Below, left:
Terrace of bluestone interspersed with water and grassy areas creates feeling of a spacious, inviting landscape.

Below, right:
Circular sandbox/fire pit is surrounded by natural plantings, in contrast with more geometric layout of paths and walls.

18 • Marc Appleton, Architect

Spectacular Long Pool Reflects Canyon Vista Beyond

California

Set just ten minutes from bustling civilization, but deep in the Topanga Canyon, this oasis-like compound is unusual in many ways. The house is open to the spectacular scenery around it, and is itself a work of unusual, eye-catching design. Influenced by a Mexican, Southwestern style, as well as a minimalist modernism, it has brightly painted exterior stucco walls, a series of walkways, courtyards and porches, terraces—and of particular interest here, a landscape with a long eye-catching lap pool.

Nestled into a sloping hillside, with magnificent views of the canyon beyond, the house and its surroundings are described as "a rural sanctuary," with its serene stucco surfaces, courtyards and corrugated metal roofs. Its design combines a touch of the old Southwestern mission in its architectural simplicity with the brilliant colors and stark forms of contemporary style. From the long rectangular central living space, French windows open onto a terrace that looks out to an adjacent meadow.

The landscape to the west includes a covered porch, an enclosed garden—and the centerpiece of the design—a dramatic sixty-foot long lap pool. Bordered by blue tiles and a series of wooden columns, the pool becomes part of the overall design of this elegant compound. The lap pool's depth and long horizontal lines, punctuated by the upright columns along one side, make it a strongly reflective and elegant addition to the compound's design.

House sits on hillside in Topanga Canyon area of California.

Colored stucco walls and minimalist forms characterize eye-catching architecture.

Spectacular 60-foot long lap pool is centerpiece of outdoor landscape.

Pool is bordered by wood columns and tile designs.

19 • Maria Smithburg, Artemesia, Landscape Architect; Tigerman McCurry, Architects

Water Canals and Outlined Lawn in Geometric Design

Colorado

Perhaps no garden and terrace in this collection bears such a resemblance to a geometric painting as this Aspen setting. Its squares and rectangles are neatly outlined and echo the windows and roof lines of this house nestled in the Colorado mountain village. Though contemporary in style, the house was designed to recall the old silver mining structures that once gave the village its Victorian character.

It has several stepped, sharply sloping metal roofs to withstand heavy snow, and wood siding with Colorado red stone used for exterior base cladding, as well as for the terrace. Numerous rectangular windows punctuate the two wings. The house is close to the street, as building codes require, and to the site's western boundary, creating space for the unusual garden, which is surrounded on its other sides by trees.

But within the space is an unusual layout: a carefully articulated geometric canal bordering the squares of red stone on the terrace, and a series of vertical and horizontal divisions, giving the area its painting-like ambiance. Reflections of sky and trees in the water add another element to the intricate design. The lawn is divided with horizontal accents and the sitting area is outlined by steel frames, providing vertical contrast to the garden's horizontals. A careful asymmetry prevails.

In this project, water is used as a geometric accent to an overall composition. as well as an element of order and serenity.

Terrace is made of squares of Colorado redstone, outlined by a water-filled canal that reflects sky and trees.

The sitting area is outlined by steel frame, providing vertical contrast to the garden's horizontal accents.

The house has two asymmetrical wings with steep sloping metal roofs to suggest original Victorian mining buildings in Aspen.

Lawns and canal are outlined to create geometric patterns.

20 • W + S Landschaftarchitekten, Conceived by Toni Weber; Kerstin Godeke, Landscape Architect

Imaginative Water Design in a Meditative, Minimalist Garden

Langenthal, Switzerland

One of the most unusual designs for a garden is this water-based minimalist setting that changes with the seasons and the snow. The dominant theme is water; it can be seen in three elements of the design in a recycled circuit on this gently hilly property.

There is an elongated canal on an upper level, a stunning "water staircase," and a large pond below. The canal acts as the water source. The water falls over the staircase, and the pond functions as the recipient. These three features are close to the main façade of the house and to a grassy lawn.

The canal, made of dark brown Corten steel sheets, creates multiple reflections of sky and landscape, which are visible from within the living room of the house. The water stairway, also made of steel, has constant heights but variable lengths for each step; the water drips gently down through row of reeds called "horse brush," which help to purify it. This is indeed an unusual and graceful sight.

Below is the pond, featuring irregular borders with plantings, and two rectilinear borders, that are defined by one small graveled terrace jutting into it, and one larger sandstone terrace near to the house. Willow trees have been planted in a free pattern, while yew hedges outline the edges of the property.

The running water and overall simplicity and minimalist character of the garden create a quiet, meditative atmosphere. On snowy days, gray and white predominate; in the growing season blue water and greenery are everywhere. A phrase by Ernst R. Hauschka inspired the philosophy of this garden design: "When we dive into our thoughts, we should not satisfy ourselves with shallow water."

Upper canal is long and narrow, and close to the house, where its reflections can be seen from the living room.

The house, pond, and waterfall steps as seen from terrace at pondside.

Dramatic water steps, the centerpiece of the design, are decorated with reeds and reflect bright colors of sky and greenery.

In snowy, icy winter, colors of steel water steps change to grays and white.

PART V: INTIMATE SPACES, COURTYARDS, AND GARDEN ROOMS

A gracious Trexas courtyard by Michael G. Imber shows how inviting small space can be. (See Chapter 21)

Many designers prefer to work with enclosed or limited outdoor spaces. Sometimes the natural terrain imposes the limits, like hillsides or brooks, near the house, and in other cases, the area is delineated by choice. Courtyards and patios are intimate areas designed for outdoor living, often cut off from the landscape beyond by the house itself, or by barriers of stone or greenery. Garden rooms are similarly enclosed spaces that may have different personalities—just like the rooms in a house—and are carefully designed with specified boundaries.

In fact, garden rooms are often seen as house additions, adding to the size of the living area—particularly in warmer climates. All of these intimate outdoor spaces provide privacy; the walls of house or garden can protect the area from the view of outsiders, as well as the view out from within. Walled outdoor rooms or patios can provide sanctuary from busy streets, as well as shelter from baking sun or heavy winds.

In all of these spaces the designer tries to balance aesthetic and practical elements, as often such small spaces are the most popular and frequently used parts of the outdoor property. Like indoor rooms these garden spaces may have real walls or natural boundaries, an elegant floor such as slate or lawn, and even a roof—of tree canopy or house overhang. Entrances, with decorative gates framing the view may add to the sense of enclosure. There are often pieces of furniture, like tables, chairs, umbrellas, and fireplaces as part of the décor.

In the following pages five projects demonstrate what can be done with intimate outdoor spaces. Each invites the owners and guests into a complete environment, not unlike a living room, but created with maximum enjoyment of the outdoors in mind.

In architect Michael Imber's Texas "cottage garden" design, a space surrounded by old oak trees (that also make a beautiful canopy "roof" for his outdoor room), is decorated with low stone walls and ornamental gateway, ceramic pots, weathered furniture, and decorative plantings. Its intimate quality is created with a series of small, irregular features, like its low stone stairway and rectangular stone well. This is an inviting garden room, both in overall design and detail.

Courtyards have a long, distinguished history as elements of outdoor design. Architect Alexander Gorlin's design for a small Memphis outdoor area takes its inspiration from the classical Italian concept of enclosed exterior space. Described as "the heart of the house," this lovely Tennessee courtyard uses geometric forms, echoing the architecture of the house, as well as greenery strategically placed to create an enclosed and intimate space.

Working with a small two-level space, architects Stephen A. Tilly and Elizabeth Martin have made two adjoining spaces into a small courtyard. Just above it—by a short set of stairs—is a woodland garden. This hillside landscape allows the visitor to enjoy both a rustic, terracotta-floored courtyard, and a picturesque wild garden with a wandering stone pathway—right in the middle of a 19th century village on the Hudson River.

Terraces are often the solution to small hillside exterior spaces. Marc Appleton combined an elegant Southern California patio space next to the house with flower-filled terraces. Winding stairs and pathways and a bridge through the terraced garden provide a lovely outdoor setting, both for outdoor living and for an inviting view from within the glass-walled house.

21 • Michael Imber, Architect

An Oak-Canopied Cottage Courtyard

Texas

When adding to a 1919 Southwestern "cottage," architect Michael Imber decided to retain the footprint of the original building, by adding vertically "to retain the cozy style." This way he was able to save the massive old oak trees that surround the house, and create a canopy for the courtyard. Not only did the new upstairs feel like a home in a tree house, but the branches of the oaks made a beautiful ceiling over the outdoor space. He described how the "eaves connect the house with the trees." The canopy of trees and a wrought-iron gate separate and enclose this intimate garden area, like the walls and doorway of an indoor room.

The charming outdoor space is creatively but subtly designed, with slight changes in levels, low stone walls, and irregular shapes—all canopied by the great oaks. A mix of natural plantings and potted plants adds to the "décor" of this outdoor room, with its weathered furniture, stone work, and ceramic objects. The overall impression is one of warm invitation, with a gentle balance between nature and careful design. This smallish space does not overwhelm the cottage next to it, in size or in formality; it is an appropriately intimate space for an almost century-old cottage.

The upstairs of the house was added to old southwestern "cottage" and canopy of oaks retained. Walls and wrought iron gate add to sense of intimacy.

Irregular steps. low walls, and stone work create inviting, enclosed space.

Ceramic pots and weathered furniture help create the sense of an "outdoor room."

Intimacy is created by roof-like canopy of trees and abundant greenery (including many ferns) and by the small, inviting spaces.

22 • Alexander Gorlin, Architect

Enclosed Garden Court Serves as an Oasis

Tennessee

A narrow, one-acre lot in downtown Memphis provides an unexpected oasis behind its street-side façade in this project designed by Alexander Gorlin. Here, a traditional open porch and vine-covered pergola with great oak trees can be seen in front of the house. A contemporary interpretation of the traditional Southern home, with a long, narrow front yard, and columned porch, there is little indication of the unusual garden courtyard behind the house. On the street side, the inviting entrance is through a wall penetrated by a wined pergola and canopy, but the outdoor living takes place behind the house.

The design "takes its inspiration from the classical Italian concept of building inward, rather than out." Here is a surprising communal living space—a courtyard that nestles between the house walls, surrounded by kitchen, living areas, and master bedroom on the ground floor. This garden court is "at the heart of the house," says the architect,, overlooked "by a series of volumes and towers and curving roofs." (The tower has an astronomical observatory in it.)

The courtyard is composed of simple geometric forms that emphasize height over width. Geometric forms, including a rectangular pool, echo design elements of the building, while the walls of the house, trees, and shrubbery provide privacy. While the project looks almost traditional from the street, the landscape behind the structure seems spacious, modern, and thoroughly up-to-date.

From street side, house in leafy neighborhood does not reveal its hidden courtyard garden.

Behind the house is "oasis" courtyard nestled into forms of the building, and echoing its geometric elements.

Functioning as "the heart of the house," and designed for communal living, the courtyard takes its inspiration from classical Italian concepts of "building in rather than out."

Entrance is through vine-covered pergola on street side of the house.

23 • Stephen A. Tilly and Elizabeth Martin, Architects

A Romantic "Rusticated" Garden for a 19th Century Village Building

New York

The past uses for this quaint, historic building in a small Hudson Valley village include several shops, the town's first movie theater, and then a playhouse, where New York productions were first tried out. Today, in its latest incarnation, it houses architectural offices, and, with an attached 19th century barn up the hill behind it, forms a U-shaped courtyard and an adjacent hillside garden.

In designing the outdoor space, the architects tried to take their "landscape cues" from the multi-level area, the 19th century architecture of the building, and from the style of many nearby gardens of immigrants from hillside towns of Italy who came to the village in the 1930s.

In the space between the playhouse and the barn is an intimate courtyard with a terracotta colored concrete floor and contrasting greenery. There is a covered stair to the garden, a story higher than the courtyard. It has an abundance of plantings and rough stone paths. It lies adjacent to the granite block wall of a section of the twenty-six-mile Croton Aqueduct. The "wild" garden has been designed in a "farm cottage" style, with a variety of densely planted flowers and shrub; among them Rugosa roses, Goat's Beard, Hollyhocks, St. John's Wort, Day Lilies, Sea Lavender, Iris, wood asters, Hosta, ivy, and Golden Alyssum. These are all plants popular in the mid 19th century.

By working with aspects of its past, the architects have brought historical continuity to the setting, as well as creating inviting and intimate spaces in the center of a village.

A 19th century building on a village street has a lovely hidden landscape behind it.

Above:
A courtyard with a terracotta colored floor provides an intimate outdoor space.

Above, right:
A steep hillside is the setting for the "cottage garden" a story higher. There are densely planted flowers with one pin oak tree among them.

Below, right:
Abundance of flowers and slate path among them help give the garden its old-fashioned charm.

24 • Marc Appleton, Architect

When the Garden is the Inspiration

California

In this unusual house-garden design, it was the garden that provided the inspiration to the architects. When the owner purchased an undistinguished 1960s tract house with a steeply sloped hillside behind it in Santa Monica, she began creating a beautiful terraced garden. The architect chose to remodel the house "in response" to the garden. He used "the traditional urban houses of Mexico and Japan" to help shape the design. "If the garden was the picture," says the architect, Mar Appleton, "the house became its frame.

He created layered walls along the street side, and opened up the interior elevations at the rear of the house of the delightful terraced garden behind. A bridge, including a long potting bench, extends the studio level outside to connect to the hillside. Contemporary windows open onto the outdoor areas, while curving stone steps rise to the different levels of the terraces. The use of curves and irregular designs of walls and pathways in the terraced garden contrasts with the modernist geometry of this side of the house.

An inviting patio is nestled between the house and garden. It is hard to picture this house as "an undistinguished suburban tract house," or the garden as simply a sloping hill; the combination of flowering hillside, nestled patio, and contemporary home shows what can be accomplished by good design in unexpected settings.

A 1960s tract house was redesigned and modernized in response to its beautiful garden, with traditional "urban houses of Japan and Mexico" to help shape the design.

House opens into inviting patio with elegant terraced garden just beyond.

Patio area nestles between house and terraced garden with bridge extending the studio level to the hillside.

Part VI: Updating Traditional Garden Styles

This elegant update on a traditional French garden design is by Hugh Dargan. (See Chapter 25)

A knowledge of world wide garden design history is of interest to many architects and designers who want to create a garden in a traditional (but updated) style—whether Japanese, Colonial Spanish, or formal French. Such designs are based on centuries of cultural and aesthetic principles. Frequently they are the "outdoor rooms" of a similarly historic house recreation. Such traditional styles suggest the philosophies or historic ideas that animated the originals—the symbolism of the Japanese garden, for example—or the ornamental geometry and careful layout of the formal gardens so beloved by French royalty.

Despite this emphasis on tradition, however, today's designs are nonetheless contemporary in many ways—from their uses of space to their carefully repeated patterns, shadows, geometric balance, and unusual plantings. And many such traditional gardens are built with ecologically sound principles.

The curious juxtaposition of modern ideas with those of distant cultures or beliefs is always fascinating. The five projects that follow explore various traditional views of garden design, and easily interpose them with the architecture of the adjoining houses.

The first design with traditional overtones is Hugh Dargan's "French chateau" garden. Separating the space into several garden rooms, the plan used many of the elements of historic French design: an alleé of plane trees, decorative gates and walls from one section to another, pruned bushes in geometric settings, and symmetrical plantings. The result is both charmingly intimate and quite formal, in keeping with the tradition of the chateau landscape.

The next project is an "Italianate" house suggested by the paintings of the great early Renaissance artist Giotto. This garden, designed by architect, Alexander Gorlin, brings to mind ancient Roman ruins. Using classical antiquity as a model, the architect has created a timeless landscape that conjures up the arches and aqueducts of two millenniums ago—an example of garden design that seems timeless.

Next we visit a Japanese garden, designed by architect Michael Glassman. This courtyard garden uses the traditional Japanese elements of stone, water, and wood; the garden is not only aesthetically pleasing, but suggest the meditative and philosophical ideas that have notably characterized Asian gardens.

The fourth example is an unusual one—a garden based on Masonic beliefs. Using the Masonic principle of the "third eye" (emphasized by an oval window with the distinctive Masonic design in the 1896 house), the architects of this contemporary garden, McIntosh Poris Associates, designed the space with symbolic Masonic ovals and appropriate symmetry.

Another project that balances tradition with contemporary ideas is Michael Imber's picturesque Spanish Colonial ranch and hunting headquarters in Texas. Using the southwest's Spanish heritage as inspiration, his building with courtyard garden and central fountain look elegant and historic, but the compound is both practical (designed for entertaining) and filled with "experimental spaces," a pool area, loggia, and other more contemporary elements.

All of these projects draw on certain cultural traditions that were indigenous to various groups, both in the United States and abroad. Like post-modern architects of the last generation, these designers have absorbed such cultural imperatives, and have made their garden spaces both evocative of another time and place, and up-to-date, as well as aesthetically pleasing.

25 • Hugh Dargan, ASLA, Landscape Architect

Garden Rooms with Old-World Charm and Present Day Uses

Georgia

The grounds of a French-style chateau are the setting for a spectacular series of garden "rooms" in a leafy section of Atlanta. In redoing the gardens to match the elegance and charm of the chateau, the designers chose to create a variety of different areas—each with its own ambiance—that would integrate the house and garden and create an appropriate sense of antiquity.

The garden is divided into four "rooms." Particularly traditional and in keeping with the French design of the chateau are the geometric and symmetrical designs, including circles and patterned squares within squares contrasted with delicate ornamentation, such as pots from Provence, and decorative ironwork railings and gates; an alleé of plane trees, antiqued stones, and topiary accents are other elements. "Distressed" stones and grass produce a checkerboard design for a "paved" area. The overall impression is simultaneously intimate and formal.

Additional areas of the garden include a circular great lawn (accented with flower beds and symmetrical plantings), a koi pond with stone steps adjacent to tennis courts, a swimming pool and pavilion, and a Zen garden and native canebrake (or thicket of cane).

Visitors to these gardens move from "room" to room, as they might within the house; the overall effect is of charm, age, and tradition.

Beautiful walled garden is entered through decorative wrought iron gates.

French-style Atlanta chateau can be seen behind walled garden.

Paving stones and grass produce a checkerboard design.

"Distressed" paving stones, with grass between them, and large planting pots from Provence add to the feeling of antiquity.

Circular grassy area is accented with flower beds and symmetrical plantings.

26 • Alexander Gorlin, Architect

Inspired by Ancient Rome: "The Inviting Gardens of an Italianate House

New York

This elegant house and studio sit on a secluded hillside in Long Island, away from the daily bustle of the resort community. In fact, the property seems to belong to another time and place—ancient Rome perhaps—immediately bringing to mind historic Italy, from its simple, fine design, to its earth-toned stucco façade, red-tiled roof, and central courtyard. Built in an L shape, with a tower at one end, and a spacious courtyard, the house was inspired by the paintings of the early Renaissance artist, Giotto. The deep, warm tones of the building provide a vibrant background for greenery—both in pots within the court, and nearby, in the garden.

It is in the garden that we find the outdoor "piece-de-resistance." Here are "the ruins," which were created from a two hundred foot long garden wall (left from a 1920s estate) with an elegant arched architectural structure bordering the pool and evoking ancient Rome's aqueducts.

Using classical antiquity as an inspiration, this garden structure creates a timeless beauty all its own. It is hard to imagine that the bustling twenty-first century is just outside the confines of this unusual site.

L-shaped house has a courtyard adorned with potted plants and central fountain.

House sits in secluded woodsy area, giving little indication of the glamorous design behind it.

Beautiful hidden pool is set deep in wooded garden with adjacent remains of old stone wall with spectacular "ruins" evoking ancient Rome.

27 • Michael Glassman, Architect

A Japanese Courtyard Garden for a U-Shaped House

California

This Japanese-inspired, low-slung wood house has a deep roof overhang and forms a U-shape—creating a perfect setting for a Japanese courtyard garden. The 20 x 40-foot courtyard fits between the two wings of the house, with the entrance in the center of the U.

The designer chose to use traditional Japanese garden components of stone, water, wood. There are small trees, shrubs, and garden sculptures. The organization of these basic elements reflects the meditative Eastern aesthetic, with each element carefully placed for design and contemplative calm.

The open side of the courtyard is fenced in wood (echoing the dark sides of the house) with alternating wide and narrow boards placed vertically. This design produces a repeating pattern of light and dark. The fence is punctuated by a large gate with its own roof, echoing the materials and roof line of the house. The gate is flanked outside the fence with a stone lantern and traditional plantings of Japanese maples, and mugo pines. An entrance path with large rocks edging it leads to the gate.

Within the courtyard an irregularly shaped pond has stepping stones and a border of flagstone in miscellaneous sizes. Water trickles slowly over the stones. The path through the pond contrasts straight lines with free-form rocks, while traditional Asian sculpture is carefully placed within the planted areas. This is a garden where little is left to chance; each element is an integral part of a concept both—both aesthetic and philosophical.

Asian sculpture and free-form rocks add to Eastern ambiance.

Traditional plantings and rocks contrast with geometric wood and stone design, with gateway echoing wood of the house.

The entrance to the Japanese -style garden is across a pond.

Japanese stone lantern marks the entrance to this appealing garden,

Trickling water is part of traditional Japanese garden aesthetic.

28 • McIntosh and Poris Associates, Architects

A Free Mason Symbol Reflected in an Oval Garden

Michigan

Several years ago an 1896 home built for a well-known Detroit artist and sculptor and member of the Free Masons, was renovated. With the help of historic photographs the Julius Melcher house and garden received a complete restoration.

The oval window at the center of the second floor became the main inspiration for the garden in front of the house. The oval window, with its central pattern, reflected Melcher's membership in the Free Masons. The symbol was known as a "third eye" or "the eye of God." In fact, Melcher's Free Masonic logo (three fish symbolizing sanctuary, warmth and hospitality) also appears in the central dormer above the doorway.

With these symbolic shapes as inspiration, the garden designers created an unusual, yet traditional landscape, in keeping with the late Victorian architecture of the Melcher house. The oval, curving pattern of mullions is replicated by a brick pathway that outlines the edges of the garden. The garden is outlined in boxwood, with an outer hedge of yew. Edging and paths are made of brick, with central sections of the walkway inset with Pewabic tile. Within the oval are fragrant Viburnum, antique roses, and Blue Speedwell. At each end of the oval is a spiral-shaped Alberta spruce.

In keeping with the symmetry in design of the 19th century house, there are two purple beech trees at either end of the house, two late flowering magnolias, and various shrubs placed symmetrically in the front garden. Low plantings include Coral bells, Black-eyed Susan, Hosta lilies, and Astilbe. Near the front door is a restored bust of Greek goddess Asheva, with the three fish of Melcher's Masonic logo carved into the bust. This is truly a garden designed with a tradition in mind.

The Julius Melcher house, built in 1896 in Detroit, features an oval window—a Masonic symbol—in the center of the second floor; it inspired the garden design.

Plantings include boxwood hedges and symmetrically placed trees and shrubbery.

A view of the oval garden in front of the house shows how the paths replicate the window design.

29 • Michael Imber, Architect •

Spanish Colonial Style for a Southwest Hunting Lodge

Texas

This picturesque ranch headquarters and hunting lodge is surely evocative of South Texas' Spanish Colonial and Mexican heritage of haciendas, presidios, and missions. Balancing the past with today's emphasis on formal design has been the aim of many architects in areas of the country with strong cultural ties to traditional design. This example brings the forms, geometry, materials, and details of Spanish archetypes to new life.

The organization of the buildings and courtyard in Texas "scrub country" act as a "foil to the nearby wilderness, with protective walls and a sentinel cistern that holds the harsh Texas surroundings at bay." There are timber and iron gates, and protective walls surrounding the lodge and its outdoor areas.

Within the compound, an elegant design unfolds: there is a long veranda, divided into private and public areas, including an outdoor dining area with views of a raised pool terrace, a fire pit, and beyond, to a spectacular lake and the wilderness. A bougainvillea-shaded loggia with a series of arches and a timbered pavilion creates an intimate outdoor space.

Built with "the hunt" in mind, this is a large place with room for entertaining and arrivals and departures through its evocative courtyard. Here the centerpiece is a splashing fountain in traditional Spanish Colonial style. This courtyard is a favorite gathering place for evening.

Outdoor dining area is shaded from Texas sun.

Courtyard has intimate proportions, with a splashing fountain as a centerpiece.

Below: Traditional Spanish colonial style and materials characterize the architecture and courtyard of this Texas lodge.

Pool reflects repeated arches of pavilion and traditional tile roof of the building.

Bougainvillea-covered loggia looks out on pool terrace and scrub country beyond.

PART VII: COMBINING FINE DESIGN, SUSTAINABLE ENERGY

Innovative "living roof" by Ted Montgomery has growing surface in the shape of a stair, and grows herbs, flowers and grasses. (See Chapter 30)

AND ENVIRONMENTAL SMARTS

One of the most interesting developments in landscape and garden design is a new—and increasingly widespread—interest in "green." While most gardens might be described as green, a few use the term to signify environmentally smart design—both for the house itself, and for the surrounding landscape.

The use of the land around the building—to help create sustainable energy within, or to further ideas of recycling (either of materials or water), or to recreate natural surroundings—is frequently combined with sophisticated design. The five projects that follow have taken environmental concerns seriously. All of them were constructed to adapt to their native climates and to be as self-sufficient as possible in terms of energy use. Instead of destroying a native habitat they attempt to preserve or recreate it, and they have used recycled materials or native materials (like trees saved from the property or local outcroppings of rock) as design elements. In terms of planting, the "green garden" uses drought-tolerant plants and effective irrigation, or recycled water in dry climates, and naturally adaptive plants in rainier areas. In water gardens, recycling takes the water on a circular journey through the garden.

Although the projects described in the section are very different from one another, each makes an environmental statement, combining good design with "green" design. (It should be noted that the projects in this section are not the only ones in this collection that are environmentally aware or eco-friendly; several such projects have been described in other sections of the book.)

The unusually attractive garden—both on the ground and on the roof of architect Ted Montgomery's house in Vermont is a prime example of eco-friendly design. Sustainable energy, replenishable materials, indoors and outdoors, and roof gardens with attractive plantings make this a unique project.

Another interesting design is one by Line and Space Architects in Arizona; it uses large overhangs over the patio for climate control in the warm desert; these overhangs help cool the environment both within the house and for outdoor areas.

A most imaginative and unusual project is in California. The Office of Mobile Design recycles surplus shipping containers, scrapped beams for building, and grain trailers to serve as koi ponds and planting areas in an unconventional and interesting design.

Another environmentally smart idea is a house with a "dog trot" by Siegel and Strain Architects. This innovation helps keep the house cool and affords a sheltered space for enjoying the outdoors in a hot climate.

And one of the most unusual—but increasingly practiced—solutions to cooling and heating a house is the project by architect Nathan Good in Oregon that is completely "green." It is a home with a vegetative roof; its garden is on top of the house.

30 • Ted Montgomery, Architect

Environmentally Sound, Aesthetically Pleasing Garden Rooms

Vermont

This architect's home and two studios are replete with gardens both indoors and out. It pays unusual attention to sustainable energy and replenishable materials, as well as to the most pleasing of garden design—replete with climbing vines, large trees, flowers, and shrubbery. A mature tree lives within the indoor garden room.

The house and studios have the newest of environmentally sound technology, with the indoor garden room providing greenery even in Vermont's cold climate. The garden room has a passive solar heating system, and among the many energy-saving features of the house are thermal mass floors, wood backup fireplaces, triple glazed glass, and salvaged building materials (including recycled windows and doors). An innovative "living roof" in the shape of a stair covers the garage; it has flowers, herbs and grasses growing on it. A four-foot high earth berm on three sides of the building helps to modulate the temperature within (in addition to reducing the visual height of the house. (As the architect, Ted Montgomery of Ground Swell Architects says, "This home resides within the landscape, emerging from the earth, rather than simply sitting on top of it.")

The indoor garden room has an 86-foot green ash tree rising through its floor—(perhaps, says the architect, the largest houseplant in the state!)—one of many such trees on the property. Ivy and grape vines climb along the walls of the unusual interior garden. This attractive space opens in warm weather onto an open wood deck over untouched earth, and an unusually intimate landscape beyond.

Among the features of the outdoor garden are a shady water garden with stone deck, vine-covered trellises and curving decorative woodwork. Plantings include numerous perennials and shrubs, vines, and many wildflowers native to Vermont fields.

Interior garden room, which can be used for 9 months of the year, has a mature green ash growing up through the floor.

Decorative wood designs add whimsical note to architecture of studio.

Intimate water garden adjoins solar-paneled garden.

Design of house and gardens works around many mature, existing trees, including bald cypress, willows, larch, Bur Oak, and lindens.

31 • Line and Space Architects

A Desert Design with Protected Outdoor Areas

Arizona

This desert house combines contemporary design with many conservation elements. Its nearby outdoor areas are covered by overhangs, both to provide a "comfort level" indoors, and a gentle transition from the brilliant sunlit exterior and darker interior space.

Situated below the high point in the foothills of the Santa Catalina Mountain ridge, it has great views of hills and desert vegetation. There are Palo Verde trees, yellow flowering Brittle Bush, and giant Saguaro cactus plants all around.

Primarily built of natural gray split face concrete block, hand split granite gathered at the site, concrete and copper, the house has large overhangs and covered patios that are shaded from the hot desert sun. As conservation issues were central to the plan, the house has two evaporatively-cooled exterior microclimates, which help cool the interior. The overhangs provide shelter from the sun as well as adding strong geometric accents to the architectural design of "solid/void massing."

The outdoor spaces around such desert houses function as protection from high winds, in addition to the sun. At the same time, the overhangs and walls create an interplay of light and shadow that adds immeasurably to the design.

Overhangs create shelter and help cool interior areas.

Both aesthetic and conservation issues are addressed with strong geometric design of desert home.

Natural growth of Saguaro cactus, mesquite trees, and Brittle Bush cover hillside near the house.

32 • Jennifer Siegal, Architect, Office of Mobile Design; Land Design by James Stone

Contemporary Design: Green, Recycled, and Chic

California

This surprising, environmentally smart, and very chic home and "oasis" garden is in an industrial area near downtown Los Angeles. Its designer, Jennifer Siegal, of the Office of Mobile Design, says she likes combining the weathered old and the shiny new, the high and the low, so that they "form a relationship."

In this unusual project she has brought together in a contemporary architectural design, shiny new glass walls and a variety of recycled junk materials in an imaginative and eco-friendly way. Situated in an old junkyard, the project takes up only one small part of a large (10,000 square foot) industrial site and is reached through a Southern California, tropical-style garden. The garden nestles against the building wall and the container structures.

Among the recycled materials are surplus shipping containers, used as part of the house itself, old grain trailers serving as koi ponds in the garden, and both wood and steel beams and roof joists that had been scrapped. These are all durable materials, which cost very little to buy or to maintain.

The project is not only interesting visually and ecologically, but it recycles an old industrial site as well.

House and garden occupy one side of industrial junkyard site near downtown Los Angeles.

House uses surplus beams and boxy cargo containers to create geometric design next to "oasis garden."

Koi ponds were constructed from recycled grain trailers.

Glass walls and recycled materials are components of this chic, environmentally innovative home.

Free-form Southern California tropical style garden nestles against wall and container structures.

33 • Siegel and Strain, Architects

KEEPING COOL WITH A DOGTROT

CALIFORNIA

This simple, linear-designed weekend house in California's wine country is the winner of a number of sustainable energy awards. Located in Sonoma County, where temperatures frequently exceed 100 degrees in summertime, it keeps itself cool with a combination of thermal mass, low-tech insulation, unusual materials (including this straw bale walls) and ceiling fans, as well as with a built-in "dog trot."

The site of the house is at the top of a sloping meadow that provides great views overlooking the vineyards below. In its immediate surroundings the house is sheltered by oak, firs, and bay trees; the building was constructed without uprooting nearby trees, and they provide a protective canopy from the sun.

But the house also has its own shelter from the hot sun: a "dog trot." This traditional design of an open, but roofed-over area between two living/sleeping wings of a house sits under a gabled roof. Cross-ventilation through the dog trot is one clue to this self-cooling house; the dog trot space is the center for outdoor living, providing a well-ventilated area for the family's activities.

Above, right:
Simple, linear design of weekend house keeps cool with innovative design, trees, and center "dogtrot."

Below, right:
House was built without uprooting nearby trees, which provide protective canopy.

Roofed-over dogtrot is cool on the hottest days in California's Sonoma valley.

Cross- ventilation is one clue to this self-cooling house; this view is from the dogtrot looking into the house.

34 • Nathan Good AIA, Architect

Award Winning "Green" Home with a Garden on the Roof

Oregon

Not many houses have flowers on the roof, or are so "green" as to require "zero energy." This unusual house faces the ocean, is surrounded by trees, and is designed "to express the owners' love of materials and forms found in nature." It is, in fact, a most original solution to combining ecological awareness with spatial design.

Built on the rugged Oregon coast, it boasts a "vegetative roof" with flowers and grass growing on it, two types of collectors to harvest sunlight for electricity and hot water, and unusual building materials, such as insulating Dirosol block. The house was sited with a nearly east/west alignment in order to better capture natural light, and the front of the house was brought forward, out from under the dark Sitka spruce nearby. Numerous additional measures in this award-winning design were taken to ensure energy efficiency.

The earth on the the roof garden is about four inches deep, with levels under it of foam insulation and fiberglass, among other materials. This grassy space keeps the house cool (and offers neighbors on the hill above an attractive view).

The small semi-circular patio overlooks a dramatic ocean view beyond, so that little is needed by way of outdoor design between the house and the sea, for nature and the clever use of technology make his a truly spectacular place.

Ocean-side, totally "green" house has two types of solar collectors, and uses ecologically sound building mateirals. Great Sitka pine is at left.

Roof garden—which aids in keeping the house cool--has grass and flowers growing on it.

There is a spectacular view of the ocean from the front picture window.

Entry to the house sits just beneath flowers growing on the roof (providing uphill neighbors with meadow-like view).

Part VIII: Combining Nature's Art with Sculpture

Two bronze cranes—Japanese symbols of long life—are set at the edge of a lily pond, amidst tall grass and stones in this garden by Martin Lee Berlinger. (See Chapter 35)

Throughout history and around the world there has been a long association between garden design and art works strategically placed. From the classical columns and statuary of gods and goddesses placed in the gardens of the ancient world to the carefully placed Buddhas of Asian gardens, to today's kinetic sculptures moving in the breeze—art has found an inviting environment surrounded by natural beauty.

Many designers consider the garden the ideal place for artworks, which both contrast with and complement the design layout and the plantings in outdoor spaces. In some cases the art takes precedence over the landscape; in others it punctuates a garden design; in some gardens it carries philosophical or religious symbolism.

Like the other elements of outdoor design, the settings for art vary tremendously—an open lawn, a fenced in corner, a bare wall, a central focal point fo a patio. While many such gardens use statuary and fountains of the past, more contemporary plans increasingly call for similarly modern art, including kinetic art and art itself made of natural garden materials.

America's history of outdoor sculpture in relation to nature must begin with cemeteries, as monuments—which became increasingly sculptural in the 19th century—have long been placed amidst trees and shrubbery. In great public cemeteries like Laurel Hill near Philadelphia and Green-Wood in Brooklyn the combination of art and landscape invited visitors to stroll on family outings to view the monuments and gracious trees.

In more recent times, as sculpture has gained tremendous popularity as an art form in the United States, sculpture parks have proliferated, with a few striving to combine elegant garden design with art.

For private homes and gardens, the placing of a single sculpture or group of statues is often a central focus point for the outdoor space. In the following projects, a few of the many solutions to the placing of art in the garden are explored. While the past tradition might have dictated the exact style and setting for garden sculpture, no such rules exist today. Styles and placements are as varied as the gardens themselves.

Designer Martin Lee Berlinger exemplifies his interest in Asian garden design with the use of statuary from Japan and Thailand throughout his garden's "rooms." He even places an Asian deity sculpture at the center of an English-style garden section. Symbolic plantings and sculpture evoke the garden's invitation to meditation, serenity, and peace.

Architect Steven Ehrlich and landscape architect Nancy Goslee Power's project is a contemporary home and garden in California, where a landscape "unfolds into a series of steps and platforms," with a rectangular reflecting pool. Strategically placed in front of a wall bordering the water are a series of sculptural forms—actually unusually shaped pieces of basalt found in a nearby quarry that function here as a form of statuary.

A most unusual project involving a form of natural sculpture is landscape architect, Gianni Biaggi's garden in Lausanne, Switzerland. In a meadow section of his garden are two giant contemporary sculptures relating to nature, and created by the designer. One, made of metal rods, aluminum foil, and pieces of mirror, represents a spider web with a man at its center. The other—also with a natural subject—suggests a giant thistle. These unusual works add an irreverent and unusual touch to the space around them.

Another California garden uses sculpture to accent a five-acre garden designed "with a modernist vocabulary of geometric forms" Art is carefully placed throughout the garden, against a white wall, surrounded by shrubbery, or standing in an open area. Here, the sculpture is an integral part of the landscape.

One of the most unusual combinations of art and landscape is the woodland garden of Jon Piasecki, both a naturalist sculptor and landscape designer. Combining his interest in ecology with design and sculpture, he has created art made of indigenous materials—stone forms, tree branches, pathways—for a most unusual and artistic landscape.

A Swiss landscape designer, Blaise Bourgeois, has created a most contemporary environment with a series of terraces and solid wooden beams laid out horizontally and interspersed with columns of pruned shrubbery that function as sculptural forms.

Each of these projects conceives of the garden as more than a compilation of plants and trees; in these examples the garden becomes a setting for art—and occasionally part of the art work itself.

35 • Marin Lee Berlinger, Creative Gardens, Landscape Designer

Symbolic Asian Art and Plantings

New York

Asian influences—both in plantings and sculpture—give Martin Lee Berlinger's garden its aesthetically pleasing design and its unusual aura of peace and contemplation. There are a number of different gardens within this seven-acre space high in the Shawanagunk Mountains of Ulster County, New York, and some acres of natural forest as well.

Each of the garden "rooms" has its own personality, many of them Asian in concept, suggesting a deep response to the mystical meanings of Eastern cultures. Each of the gardens has symbolic plantings or designs, some with the running water or raked stones familiar to devotees of Japanese gardens, other with more Western design, but nonetheless ornamented with Asian statuary.

This surprising mix of East and West, as well as the fusion of several different Asian elements, makes Berlinger's gardens interesting and inviting. But these gardens are also symbolic in many ways, with the use of particular plants, settings, and sculpture to suggest Feng-shui (the Chinese principles of imperceptible energies) with various Asian deities (Japanese and Thai), symbolizing peace and serenity. Typical of the symbolic plantings in this garden is a carefully pruned cedar tree that suggests clouds, and raked gravel representing the sea.

The gardens are not dramatic statements; they are complete, small-scale environments. One is an English perennial garden filled with colorful flowers in precisely delineated growing beds, punctuated by an Asian statue. Another is a Thai garden with a teahouse. A third has tall, exotic grasses with an asymmetrically shaped stone-edged gold fishpond and pagoda, with delicate gates handmade from fallen trees. The small Asian deities and stone benches are often hidden among the shrubbery. One garden "room" has two stone islands, one symbolizing a turtle, the other a crane (representing wisdom and long life) floating in a "sea" of gravel and surrounded by a fence or redwood, cedar and bamboo. In all of these gardens, art is an integral part of the design and a symbolic reminder of mystical principles.

English-style garden has centerpiece of Thai sculpture (the legendary King Phaapaimanee, who stopped a war with his flute playing).

Asian garden, with raked gravel and carefully set stones and statuary, typifies aura of meditation and harmony.

Thai teahouse is adorned with bronze statue in position of prayer.

Bronze fountain is surrounded by three dolphins shooting water; it was made in Bangkok in a European style.

36 • Steven Ehrlich, Architect; Nancy Goslee Power, Landscape Architect

Cubes, Angles, and "Statuary" in a Contemporary Setting

California

This geometrically styled house in shades of neutral and white stucco sits on a sloping corner lot. The interior includes large open spaces, including a 2500 square foot studio. The design of the house, with its "dance of cubic volumes and vertical stucco masses with cantilevered roof planes" is echoed by the landscape design, as it seems to "unfold into a series of steps and platforms." These floating planes of stone extend into the front and rear gardens as stairs and transitional platforms. They terminate behind the house in a reflecting pool accented with sculpture.

The zigzag entrance design, made of sweetwater sandstone, is punctuated by plantings of rosemary, juniper, and ginkos, as well as by some small statuary. The designers described the complex front design as a way to distance the house from a busy street scene, in effect creating an illusion of great space with its white horizontal patterns.

Another side of the house has a series of walks at different levels and in different shades of stucco. An unusual feature of the house is the use of "rain chains," borrowed from an old Japanese technique, which draw water from the roof downward into the garden.

In the back of the house is a striking area of what seems to be sculpture set in a low, watery, oblong pool. Inspired by the works of Isamu Noguchi, according to the landscape designer, this attractive feature actually consists of natural, unusually shaped pieces of basalt found in a quarry near Ventura, California, and set against a pinkish stucco wall. These interesting elements function as strong sculptural accents.

Corner view of house includes cantilevered sheet metal roof with column and "rain chains."

Entrance and front façade of house creates geometric patterns with stairs and landings; landscape design too "unfolds" into a series of steps and platforms."

Side of the house uses various subtle shades of stucco in both house and walls surrounding it.

Behind the house is an oblong area of shallow water punctuated by natural pieces of basalt that function as sculptural forms.

37 • Gianni Biaggi, Landscape Architect

A Swiss Garden Combining Tradition and Imaginative Sculpture

Lausanne, Switzerland

There are many dualities and contrasts in this extraordinary garden: meadows and cultivated lawn, carefully placed pergola and arbor vs. free-form growing areas, natural plantings vs. man-made sculpture. The sloping terrain was designed to create both a large meadow and a terraced lawn, separated by a stone wall on one side, and flower beds and granite pathway on the other.

The lawn is trapeze-shaped to create an illusion of greater depth. At one end are a periwinkle–covered pergola, a greenhouse, and a shed. Near the house are a stone terrace and a small natural pond connected to a fountain, and a brook "to create a transversal axis." Plantings include an abundance of bulbs, annuals, and perennials, including roses and climbers, and even potted plants moved from the greenhouse to the garden.

An unusual feature is the contrast to the tended garden created by two giant contemporary sculptures: one represents a thistle "evoking the duality of nature and culture," and the other "a spider web with a man at the center." The latter is made of metal rods, aluminum foil and mirror pieces "to imprison the silhouette of man." Both are by the garden's designer.

The architect comments that the garden is meant to change over time, and in different seasons, despite its basic elements and vistas.

Above, right:
Profusely planted garden includes pond and rose-covered arbor.

Below, right:
A granite-slab pathway leads through the greenery to the house.

Giant thistle sculpture sits in flower-covered meadow.

Spider-web sculpture has silhouette of a man in it, signifying "his imprisonment in his destiny."

38 • Rios, Clementi, and Hale Studios, Landscape Architects

Contemporary Sculpture Enhances a Garden Design

California

With a modernist house design and materials as inspiration, landscape architects at Rios, Clementi, and Hale Studios conceived of a garden that merged the contemporary and the surrounding naturalistic setting of mixed terrain, including the arroyo nearby. The five-acre garden was laid out with "a modernist vocabulary of geometric forms," (much like the house), and enhanced with artwork.

The use of art to punctuate a landscape has a long tradition; contemporary sculpture is particularly well-suited to large outdoor spaces. Its often large or kinetic forms are best appreciated with the space, colors, and shapes of nature around them. In this garden the designers used sculpture with a "minimal plant palette" near the house, and series of smaller garden area: shade gardens, succulent gardens, and other plant ecosystems—interspersed with the straight and curving lines of walls, pathways, and stairs.

The art appears along a white wall in two-dimensional form, and in a large free-standing work called "Square Root of Two" by contemporary artist, Mark DiSuvero, in an open area. Both pieces are colorful and abstract, contrasting with the more traditional garden elements, and providing another aesthetic dimension to the visual beauty of the landscape.

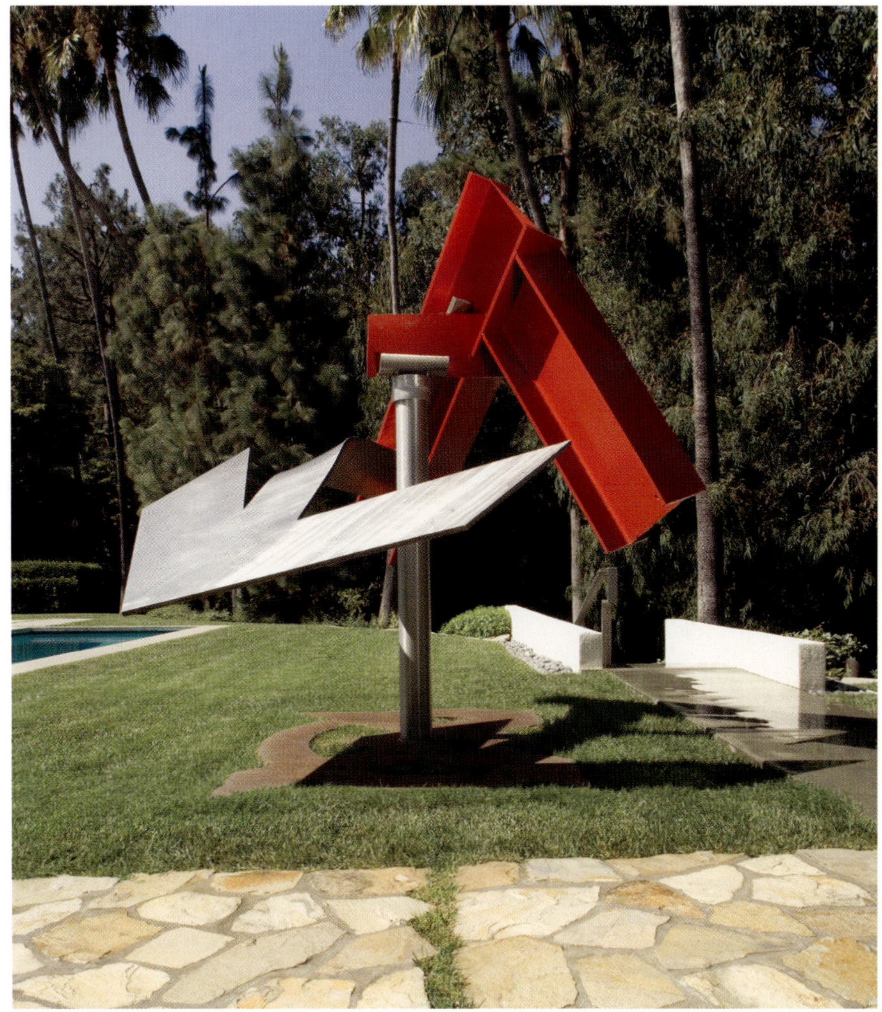

Free-standing sculpture "Square Root of Two" by Mark diSuvero sits in open area; its geometric shapes reflecting modernist house and contrasting with nature's forms nearby.

Rectangular forms and horizontal lines of house are reflected in the shape of the lily pond.

Nearby is a more natural area with curving steps and old stone walls.

Above:
Garden and pool echo both forms and stonework of the house.

Below:
Two-dimensional art work enhances stone wall.

39 • Jon Piasecki of Golden Bough, Landscape Architect

A Naturalist Sculptor Designs a Landscape

New York

The house has a mica schist path and high bush blueberry hedge.

Combining his interest in landscape architecture, history, forest ecology, Bronze Age stonework, and sculpture made of "found" materials, Jon Piasecki has created a most unusual site. Located in New York State's Columbia County, this woodland area has yielded many Native American treasures, as well as natural rock outcroppings amid a forest of trees (none of which were cut down to create the landscape).

Piasecki likes to call his view of landscape design a "do no harm approach." He saves the landscape, uses mostly indigenous plants (and avoids bringing heavy equipment into the area.) His organic process is carefully structured to "connect people ecologically and culturally to the land."

His project for this property involved creating paths through the forest surrounding the house, and a landscape combining nature and art. In creating such paths through the woods, he discovered mysterious piles of rocks and Indian artifacts, which helped inspire some of this sculpture, including the large piles of stone stacked among the trees. Composed of mossy stone arranged around a multi-stemmed red oak, these sculptures are described by the designer as "trail markers." Other smaller stones are used as parts of a mobile, with some hundred individual pieces dangling from tree branches.

The forms of tree limbs create another of Piasecki's natural sculptures; fallen branches are formed into a great hanging wood sculpture in a small clearing in the forest. Neatly laid out hornbeam branches also form a bridge through a wetland area.

Throughout the woodlands art and nature have a strikingly comfortable relationship; the use of natural materials and the spatial dimensions of the sculpture within the landscape make this a fully integrated project, reflecting both contemporary taste and fascination with the distant past. "I want to give new life to forgotten things," says Piasecki.

Suspended sculpture, created with fallen branches, is placed in woody area.

Piles of rocks, which designer calls "trail markers" suggest mysterious stone piles left by Native Americans.

40 • Blaise Bourgeois of Oxalis, Landscape Architect

When Nature Takes Sculptural Forms

Geneva, Switzerland

In a striking and unusual garden in the countryside near Geneva, art and architecture and nature are joined together in an unusual alliance. Here nature's forms become sculptural, and the horizontal architecture of the house is echoed by linear sculptural design in the garden.

The concept of this garden includes "dialogues between the rooms of the house and the various garden spaces." In fact, the designer has used nature and art to continue the lines and forms of the house, with horizontal areas of lawn articulated by a series of turfed terraces and three long, solid wooden beams in the ground—all echoing the architectural lines of the house.

Nature itself, in the guise of columns of pruned hornbeams, is used to give the illusion of a series of sculptural forms. At the entrance to the property a corridor affect is created by a great horizontal wall and hedge. This corridor leads to the pruned hornbeams, in effect forming an architecture of nature, with the topiary-like columns of greenery appearing to resemble to standing group of statues.

The property is divided into several areas. The north garden suggests open space; its lawn vista is occasionally broken by a hornbeam (or another sculptural form), and its distant boundary is a screen of willows. This curtain of trees (which vibrates in the light) creates a division between it and the south garden, which is more playful, with a pool, a vegetable garden, terraces, and flowerbeds. This is a thoughtful and original use of garden space that uses abstract forms and perspective to unify house and garden.

Hornbeam bridge crosses wetland area in this most unusual landscape.

View from the living room with its own sculpture, shows north garden with its architectural characteristics.

Part IX: Defining Space with Pergolas, Arches,

Architect Elizabeth Thompson's use of woven fir lattice in deck and gazebo creates wonderful patterns of sun and shadow. (See Chapter 41)

Gazebos, and Fences

Many contemporary garden areas are defined by interesting structures, whether of wood or stone or cement, or a combination of materials. Such structures can separate garden spaces from one another and create intimate spaces. They also allow a variety of uses for different sections of a garden, such as a dining space, or an entranceway, or a transitional area from one part to another. But their major function is to impose a kind of order on the garden composition—a way of organizing the natural wildness of a landscape. In a visual sense, garden structures can complement their surroundings, provide geometric accents to amorphous plantings, or frames to the garden view.

The wooden deck bridges the indoor-outdoor separation, allowing the enjoyment of the garden from a slightly raised, cleanable surface, while forming a transition to the garden area. The pergola, while originally designed to facilitate picking fruit and providing shade, is today mostly a design element—often planted with climbing vines or bougainvillea. Trellises and arbors are similarly designed to enhance the layout of the garden, and to provide vertical accents to a flat space.

Such small structures have a long history from ancient pergolas to today's sophisticated decks, summer houses, and outdoor patio designs. Their practical uses, as well as their aesthetic contribution to the landscape make them ever more popular. As people spend more and more time outdoors for eating and entertaining and simply relaxing, the small garden structure has become a welcome addition. Some are rustic, others more urban-looking, and many take their design elements from the style of the house they adjoin.

One of the most popular materials for garden structures is wood—long used for trellises, pergolas, and walkways. Contemporary versions of these traditional structures include geometric abstractions with complex latticework providing interesting sun and shade patterns. Even picket fences can be used in a variety of patterns to create complexity of design. Many garden structures are of whimsical design, whether for practical use like (storage areas), or for purely aesthetic reasons.

Stone and cement are also common materials for garden structures. Columns and stanchions relate directly to ancient design, while carefully placed stonewalls and walkways can show Asian influences. Many stone structures are made of indigenous stone found nearby. Frequently, materials like these match those used in the house exterior, thus relating the garden design directly to the architecture.

In the following examples, imaginative use of garden structures adds immeasurably to the design of outdoor space and to the quality of outdoor life for the residents of the house. In fact, each project shown here brings the architecture of the house into the garden in interesting ways.

In Elizabeth Thompson's delightful gazebo and deck design, the area is open to sun and breezes. But at the same time, this design makes an architectural statement of its own with its geometric construction and airy latticework.

The beautiful garden designed by Stefan Thuilot is organized with an elegant combination of structures, water, and plantings. The structures provide a sense of composition that is defined by geometry and color within a very inviting space next to the house.

With the use of wooden fencing and a pergola planted with ivy, architect Peter Kurt Woerner took a small space and created a pair of courtyards and an interesting visual division of a narrow garden area. This is an example of using wood to break up and impose design on an otherwise undistinguished area.

The next project is another example of a charming gazebo that adds to the ambiance and practical uses of a deck. Overlooking a small tributary creek with a tranquil wildlife refuge that borders the house, the gazebo provides a screened outdoor "room" for the house, in addition to wonderful views of willows and wildlife.

A rhythmic design of light and shadow characterizes architect Chris Schmitt's innovative wooden walkway in a South Carolina project. Using pressure-treated pine, the architect made porches, decks and walkways, and a pergola that bring in the natural light and beauty of the salt marsh landscape.

Each of these examples suggests the limitless opportunities available to the designer in even the smallest spaces. Small structures like these can be the component parts of the redesigned garden—the "user-friendly" additions that make the outdoor "rooms" of the garden inviting and intimate, as well as aesthetically elegant.

41 • Elizabeth Thompson, Architect

Whimsical Gazebo Complements a Japanese Garden

Maryland

The use of wood as a design element is central to the deck, gazebo, and garden created by architect Elizabeth Thompson. The house has a deck with a bench along its railing and a zig-zag pattern of flooring. This design culminates in a dream-like gazebo, open to sun and breeze, with an architectural integrity of its own.

Made of woven fir lattice-work, the gazebo is "whimsical and light-spirited, creating dancing patterns of light and shadow on the deck below," says the designer. Using an equilateral triangular framework atop a pentagonal floor, the gazebo resembles a delicate geometric model. A series of straight lattice strips are laid across the frames in opposite directions, to create six "hyperbolic-paraboloid shapes," and to form a ceiling and walls for the gazebo. The surprising design of this gazebo is a wonderful and original addition to the garden.

In growing season flowering clematis vines weave through the lattice work (and attract hummingbirds). Just beyond the deck and gazebo are plantings in the Japanese tradition. This is truly an inviting space for enjoying the out-of–doors; the designer comments that an afternoon in the gazebo is "hard to surpass as a place for an afternoon cup of tea."

Gazebo adorns wood deck adjacent to Japanese -style garden.

The architect describes the setting of deck and gazebo as "hard to surpass for an afternoon cup of tea".

Geometric structure and lattice work patterns of gazebo create brilliant designs of light and shadow.

42 • Stefan Thuilot with Joseph Huettl, Huettl-Thuilot Associates, Landscape Architects

Defining Structures in a Design for Outdoor Living

California

With this award-winning garden, designer Stefan Thuilot shows what can be done with the careful organization of a small space. In building a variety of structures and walkways, he imposes organization and geometric design, while allowing lush vegetation throughout.

The focal point of the space is the outdoor eating area, defined by a wood trellised pergola with a latticed roof, as well as cement columns, and a striking contemporary fireplace. Leading up to this area is a redwood walkway, bordered by pink coral bells and low white stucco walls. On the opposite side of the garden, a tranquil series of lily ponds and a bluestone patio have as the focal point a copper backed fountain This unusual element is surrounded by delicate natural reeds and low white walls. The entire layout creates a meditative beauty, influenced, in addition, by the style of the Asian gardens.

The overall effect of these structures of different materials is to provide a painting-like organization of the space, with verticals and horizontals creating patterns throughout, softened by the natural flowers and shrubbery. This garden demonstrates how a small space may give the impression of being larger with the imposition of a series of design elements and structures than if it is left open and empty. Not only does the design of this space have a visual beauty, but it provides an elegant and practical setting for outdoor living.

Plant-bordered red wood walkway leads to pergola and contemporary fireplace.

Inviting eating area is defined by columns and latticed roof, while small lily pond areas are placed within bluestone paving.

Beautifully designed lily ponds are delineated by geometric design in contemplative area of garden.

Fountain has copper back and is surrounded by combination of natural reeds and walls.

43 • Peter Kurt Woerner. Architect

An Old Meeting Hall's Garden Gets a Makeover

Connecticut

Turning a flat-roofed, concrete block, former V.F.W. meeting hall into a cheerful apartment building required both interior and exterior renovation. Additions to the exterior included a Greek Revival pediment and portico (to echo the architecture on this 19th century block) on the street side, and an unusual makeover behind the building. In the interior, what was once one large room became two apartments with walkout private courtyards on the lower level, and loft apartments above.

Behind the building a series of ingenious fences, stairs, retaining walls and a central pergola (leading to a parking space) turned a nondescript area into an unusual design. The new set-up has two private courtyards for the tenants. The area around the buildings and courtyards were planted with ivy, to remain green year-round, and the entire complex was enclosed with a gently curving fence.

This project is an example of how the addition of small structures—fencing, stairs, courtyards, and pergola can both give an undistinguished area an entirely new ambiance, and create privacy and charm for the residents.

Former meeting hall was renovated into a four-apartment house with new exterior architectural details and white picket fence.

Gently curving fence encloses hidden courtyards within the compound.

Ingenious collection of fences, stairs, and central pergola adjoin private courtyards.

44 • Designed by Stephen Ahlf and Owner

Waterside Gazebo Overlooking A Wildlife Refuge

New York

Perched high over a picturesque tributary of the Hudson River, this screened gazebo feels like a tree house. Branches of a nearby black willow tree surround the deck and gazebo, providing privacy and shade, while down below waterfowl and fish can be seen in and around the creek. Once a major water route inland for goods from sailing ships arriving on the Hudson, this narrow waterway is now a wildlife refuge with a natural habitat for birds.

The house with a deck on three sides was built in the 1980s. The structure sits on a narrow spit of land between the road and edge of the creek. Some years later the gabled gazebo was added to create an "outdoor room" for dining, entertaining, and even watching television on a warm evening. The pressure-treated wood gazebo (measuring 13 and one half feet by almost 10 feet) has screened sides all around. It has both electricity and telephone, and even in the warm Hudson valley summers, breezes pass right through it.

The gazebo was built onto a corner of the deck, with steel supports going down to the ground level below. It has generous roof overhangs so it can even be used during rain storms, and deep window sills. It is even has screening under the floor, so mosquitoes cannot find their way in. The combination of deck and gazebo provides a high, waterside view of nature, and an inviting setting for entertaining.

Below:
Simple interior of screened gazebo shows water below and branches of black willow tree all around.

House and deck with gazebo are high above Hudson River tributary known as "The Creek," now a nature sanctuary.

Gable-roofed gazebo is perched high in the trees, overlooking water below.

45 • Chris Schmitt of Schmitt Walker Architects and Thomas Angell, Landscape Architect

Innovative Wooden Constructions near a Salt Marsh

South Carolina

A former rice plantation in South Carolina (where Robert E. Lee got his start) is the setting for this residential compound of four separate buildings, a central garden, and a series of innovative wooden structures. The house was designed by Chris Schmitt, who turned to Thomas Angell of Verdant Enterprises for landscape design. The designers chose to link both the buildings and the wild natural salt marsh landscape—live oak trees, pond, and fields—with wooden designs that fit gracefully into the landscape. Among these structures are walkways, pergolas, porches, and decks made of pressure treated pine.

The buildings of the compound include a house, a studio/ greenhouse, a storage shed, and a garage (with space for kayaks). There is a planted flower garden too, but most of the property is left in its wild, natural state. The central living space in the house opens onto a deck with a pool that has the natural landscape on one side and the cultivated garden, bordered by a curving wall on the other. The pond just beyond the pergola is kept flooded as a natural habitat for water birds.

There are two pergolas. The design of the long pergola with its repeated open spaces creates a dramatic pattern of light and shadow with its latticework; one side is also adorned with vines. The designers describe the other pergola as forming "a transition to the live oaks and the pond." Decks and porches (some of which are screened) also allow the residents to feel closer to the beauty of the surrounding salt marsh and great trees.

The view from within the partially roofed and sided walkway has pattern created by light and spacing of wood construction. Vines adorn the side.

Curving brick wall edges garden planted with flowers indigenous to South Carolina salt marsh areas.

The salt marshes lie just beyond the footpath and bridge.

One pergola stretches into natural landscape toward the pond, which is kept flooded for water birds.

The cedar-shingled house has a series of decks and pergolas attaching four separate structures.

List of Architects and Designers

Thomas Angell
Verdant Enterprises
P.O. Box 77
Waterboro, SC 29488
tel: 843-549-6622

Marc Appleton
Appleton and Associates Inc.
1556 17th Street
Santa Monica, CA 90404
tel: 310-828-0430

Martin Lee Berlinger
Creative Gardens
189 Bush Street
Stone Ridge, N.Y. 12484
web: www.creative-gardens.biz

Gianni Biaggi
Avenue Charles Secretan, 25
1005 Lausanne, Switzerland
tel: 021-22-16-44

Blaise Bourgeois, N. Ferraud,
and H. Kikuchi
Oxalis Architectes Paysagistes
Rue de Veyrier, 19
1227 Carouge (GE), Switzerland
web: www.oxalis-landscape.ch

Milford Cushman
The Cushman Design Group, Inc.
P.O. Box 655, 100 Mountain Road
Stowe, VT 05672
tel: 802-253-2169
web: www.cushmandesign.com

Mary Palmer Dargan, ASLA,
and Hugh Dargan, ASLA
3091 Maple Drive
Suite 206
Atlanta, GA 30305
tel: 800-454-3889
web: www/dargan.com

Steven Ehrlich Architects
10865 Washington Blvd.
Culver City, CA 90232
tel: 310-838-9700
web: www/s-ehrlich.com

Michael Glassman
719 56th Street
Sacramento, CA 95819
tel: 916-736-2222

Nathan Good Architect PC
1586 Aloha Court
Salem, OR 97302
tel: 503-370-4448
web: www.NathanGoodArchitect.com

Alexander Gorlin Architects
137 Varick Street
New York City, NY 10013
tel: 212-229-1199
web: www.alexandergorlinarchitects.com

Hanrahan Meyers Architects
135 West 20th St.
New York City, NY 10011
tel: 212-989-6026
web: www.hanrahanmeyers.com

Christoph Husler
Husler Architectes-Paysagistes
Rue de L'Ale, 30
1003 Lausanne, Switzerland
web: www/huslerpaysagistes.ch

Michael G. Imber
Michael G. Imber Architects
111 West El Prado
San Antonio, TX 78212
tel: 210-824-7703

Grace Kennedy
Grace Kennedy Garden Design
832 Route 9D
Garrison, NY 10524
tel: 845-424-3409
web: www.gracekennedygardendesigcom

Scott Lindenau AIA and Kevin Heath AIA
Studio B Architects
555 N. Mill Street
Aspen, CO 81611
tel: 970-920-9428
web: www.studiobarchitects.net

Line and Space, LLC
627 East Speedway
Tucson, AZ 85705
tel: 520-623-1313
web: wwwlineandspace.com

Gavin Macrae-Gibson
Macrae-Gibson Architects P.C.
450 Seventh Avenue
New York City, NY 10001
tel: 212-294-2940; web:m-ga.com

Donald Mallow Architect
103 Glenwood Avenue
Leonia, NJ 07605
tel: 201-947-1510
web: www.donaldmellow.com

McIntosh Poris Associates
36801 Woodward Suite 200
Birmingham, MI 48009-9346
tel: 248-258-9346
web: www.mcintoshporis.com

Steve Mensch Architect
215 Mill Road
Rhinebeck, NY 12572
tel: 845-876-6238

Sigrid Miller-Pollin, AIA Architecture
1290 South East Street
Amherst, MA 01002
tel: 413-549-2007
web: www.millerpollin.com

Ted Montgomery Architect
477 Ten Stones Circle
Charlotte, VT 05445
tel: 802-425-7707

Juergen Partridge Architect
16012 Shaws Creek Road
Caledon, Ontario L76 1V7 Canada
tel: 905-838-1983 or 1-800-341-6656
web: www.partridgedesign.com

Jon Piasecki
Golden Bough Landscape Architecture
276 N. Plain Road
Housatonic, MA 01236
tel: 413-274-6243

Carol Pope
Landscape Design
119 High Street
Amherst, MA 01002

Nancy Goslee Power Asso.
1660 Stanford Street
Santa Monica, CA 90404
tel: 310-264-0266
web: www.nancypower.com

Antoine Predock Architect
Albuquerque Studio
300 12th Street NW
Albuquerque, NM 87102
tel: 505-843-7390

Rios Clementi Hale Studios
Landscape Architects
6824 Melrose Avenue
Los Angeles, CA 90038
tel: 323-634-9220

Chris Schmitt
Schmitt Walker Architects
12-A Vanderhorst Street
Charleston, SC 29403
tel: 843-727-3140
web: www.schmittwalker.com

Jennifer Siegal, Architect
Office of Mobile Design
1725 Abbot Kinney Blvd.
Venice, CA 90291
tel: 310-439-1129
web: www.designmobile.com

Siegel and Strain Architects
1295 59th Street
Emeryville, CA 94608
tel: 510-547-8092
web: www.siegelstrain.com

Maria Smithburg, Landscape Architect
Artemesia
132 East Delaware # 6002
Chicago, IL 60611
tel: 312-654-1708

Elizabeth Thompson, Architect
250 Mercer Street

New York City, NY 10012
tel: 212-614-7180
web: www.elizabeththompsonarchitect.com
Stefan Thuilot

Stefan Thuillot
Huettl and Thuilot Associates, Landscape Architects
1250 Addison Street Suite 212
Berkeley, CA 94702
tel: 510-548-3200

Tigerman McCurry, Architects
444 N. Wells Street
Chicago, IL 60610
tel: 312-644-5880

Stephen Tilly and Elizabeth Martin, Architects
22 Elm Street
Dobbs Ferry, NY 10522
tel: 914-693-8898

Toni Weber, Kerstin Godeke, Landscape Architects
W + S Landschaftsarchiteckten
Untere Steingrubenstrasse 19
4500 Solothurn SW, Switzerland
web: www.greenconcept.ch
landschaftarchitekten-BSLA.html

Peter Kurt Woerner, Architect
group c. inc
514 Chapel Street
New Haven, CT 06511
tel: 203-777-0002
web:www.groupcinc.com

Photography Credits

All photographs are courtesy of the architects and designers, except the following:

Chapter 1: Photography by Norman McGrath

Chapter 4: Photography by Paul Warchol

Chapter 6: Photography by Timothy Hursley

Chapter 10: Photography by Susan Allen

Chapter 14: picture #1 photography by Peter Mauss / ESTO

Chapter 16: Photography by Carolyn Bates

Chapter 18: Photography by Alex Vertikoff

Chapter 22: Photography by Albert Vecerka/ ESTO

Chapter 23: Photography by Steve Gunther

Chapter 25: Photography by Mary Palmer Dargan

Chapter 26: Photography by Michael Moran

Chapter 28: Photography by Kevin Bauman

Chapter 31: Pictures #1,2,3 photography by Henry Tom

Chapter 32: Pictures # 1, 4, 5: photography by Undine Prohl; pictures #2,3 photography by Benny Chan

Chapter 34: picture # 2: Photography by Dan Morrison

Chapter 36: Photography by Juergen Nogai

Chapter 38: Photography by Tom Bonner

Chapter 43: Photography by Karen Bussolini

Chapter 44: Photography by Robert Samuels